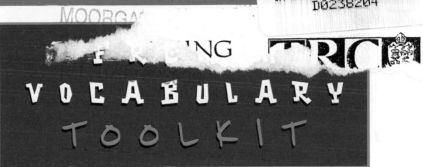

FRENCH VOCABULARY TOOLKIT

CONTENTS

Welcome to the French Vocabulary Toolkit!

The aim of this book is to help you to learn the vocabulary which you will need to do well in the GCSE examination in French. The vocabulary listed in the book is based on the word lists in the specifications of the Assessment and Qualifications Alliance (AQA), London Examinations (Edexcel) and Oxford, Cambridge and RSA Examinations (OCR). Your teacher will tell you which awarding body you are using.

You will not be allowed to use a dictionary in your examinations, so it is important that you have a good knowledge of vocabulary to back you up. The more words you know, the easier you will find it to do the questions well. Just as you can't build a house without bricks, you can't write in French without the words to put into the sentences.

Structure of the book

This book is arranged in topics, which cover the topics required by the Specifications. The titles are given at the beginning of each section. In addition, each section uses colour to show the gender of the nouns. Masculine nouns are printed in blue (un/le); feminine nouns are printed in red (une/la). Verbs are printed in green. All other types of word are printed in black. (There is some evidence to show that colour coding helps one remember which gender group a word belongs to by picturing the colour groups on the page.) An asterisk (*) denotes vocabulary more likely to appear at Higher level.

The activities

After the list of words in each topic, there are a number of activities which will help you check whether you have learned the words. You should only do these activities when you have finished learning the vocabulary.

It would be possible to do the activities by writing the answers into the book, but it would be much better to write your answers onto a separate piece of paper. You could then do the activities several times – the more often you use the words the better they will become fixed in your memory. You will also be able to revise as the exam approaches.

Maybe you have bought the book a few weeks before the examination! In this case, do the exercises first. This will help you to find out which words you know and which ones you need to learn.

You will find the answers to the activities at the back of the book. Only look at the answers once you have done the exercises! Then you will find out which words you really have learnt. Don't look first! It won't help you to learn the words; it will only make you think that you know more than you really do.

You may have some answers which are different from the ones provided. This could well be the case. Don't automatically assume that you are wrong. Check with your teacher to see if your answer is also possible. (Maybe you could write to us at Collins and we could include your answers in a future edition!)

Vocabulary learning

Vocabulary learning is an essential part of learning a foreign language and there are no short cuts. You have to build up your vocabulary by learning it slowly and gradually. Good linguists have a large vocabulary.

If you manage to learn ten words every day from Monday to Friday and use the weekend to revise them, you will learn 50 words a week. If you learn 50 words a week, you will learn 200 words in a month. 200 words every month means that you learn 2400 in a year. And 2400 words is more than enough for GCSE!

People learn vocabulary in different ways. You need to find the way which is best for you and use it regularly. In the next section we give you some tips on how to learn vocabulary. Try some of them out and you may find that learning vocabulary is more fun than you thought it was.

Amuse-toi bien!

Tips on vocabulary learning

1   Keep this book with you all the time. Use it when you have a spare moment. Every little helps! Test yourself regularly. Tick the words you really do know and concentrate on the ones you need to learn.

2 Use this book often: while you are waiting for the bus; on the bus; when you have a few minutes to spare at home.

3 Write out the words which you are finding difficult to learn. Write them slowly and carefully. Write them four or five times each.

4 Keep a separate notebook for words which you come across which are not in this book. Use this note book in the same way: go through it regularly, so that you learn these words too. The more words you know, the easier you will find it to do the tests in the examination.

5 Make a set of vocabulary cards. Write the English word on one side of the card and the French word on the other. Go through the cards, testing yourself on the words. Put the words you know to one side. If you don't know a word, put it at the bottom of the pack, so that it comes up again until you really do know it.

6 Get your parents, a relation or a friend to test you on the words you have to learn. It doesn't matter if they don't speak French. If they aren't sure if you got the word right, get them to ask you to spell it.

7 Write down the words on little notes and put them around the house in places where you will see them regularly, e.g. by the television; in the bathroom; on the stairs; by the computer; by your bed; on the fridge. Tell your parents this is a vital part of your learning for GCSE!

8 Use your vocabulary cards in the same way. Put one by the front door. Every time you come in or go out, look at the English word, say the foreign word, then turn the card over to see if you got it right. When you are sure you know the word, change the card for another one.

9 Say the words out loud when you are learning them. It helps you to remember them.

10 Make a cassette to help you learn the words. Write down a list of the English words and the French words. Speak the English words out loud one by one onto the cassette. After each English word, say the French word to yourself twice, without speaking out loud. This leaves a gap on the tape. When you have finished, play the tape and try to say the foreign word in the gap on the tape. When you can do this quickly for all the words, you will have learnt them. You can use the tape on your walkman.

11 If you are having difficulties remembering a word, ask a friend (or a teacher) to ask you what it is every time they pass you in the corridor. Make it into a kind of joke. You'll soon learn it then!

12 And don't forget to try and learn a small number of words each day. Remember: 10 a day = 50 a week = 200 a month = 2400 a year.

Success at GCSE!

A note to parents

You can help your son or daughter by supporting them in their vocabulary learning. Even if you don't speak French, you can probably tell whether they know the word or not. If you are not sure, ask your son or daughter to spell it.

Allow your child to put some of the vocabulary learning tips into practice. It may mean having a lot of notes around your home and will make dusting difficult for a while – but you will be pleased when your child passes GCSE!

Take an interest in their vocabulary-learning and encourage them to do it. Try to have a regular time each day (e.g. after a meal) when you listen to the words they have learnt. Most children need a structure to help them learn. You can provide that.

un adulte	adult	le frère	brother
l'âge	age	le garçon	boy
un agent de police	police officer	les grands-parents (pl)	grandparents
un ami	friend		
un an	year	*le jumeau	twin
un animal (pl: animaux)	animal/pet	le lapin	rabbit
		le mari	husband
un anniversaire	birthday	*le neveu	nephew
*le beau-frère	brother-in-law	le nom	(sur)name
*le beau-père	step-father, father-in-law	un oiseau	bird
		un oncle	uncle
le bébé	baby	*un orphelin	orphan
le caissier	check-out operator	un ouvrier	workman
		les parents (pl)	parents
le camarade (de classe)	(class) mate	le perroquet	parrot
le chat	cat	le poisson (rouge)	(gold) fish
le chauffeur	driver	le prénom	first name
le cheval (pl: chevaux)	horse	le professeur	teacher
		*le troisième âge	old age
les cheveux (pl)	hair	le vendeur	salesman
le chien	dog	le voisin	neighbour
le cobaye	guinea-pig	les yeux (pl)	eyes
le copain	friend/mate		
le correspondant	pen-friend	une amie	friend
*le cousin	cousin	l'amitié	friendship
*le demi-frère	half-brother, step-brother	une année	year
		la barbe	beard
un employé de bureau	office worker	*la belle-mère	step-mother, mother-in-law
un enfant	child		
*un époux	husband	la copine	friend
le facteur	postman	la cousine	cousin
le fils	son		

*la demi-sœur	half-sister, step-sister	*se marier	to get married
la famille	family	présenter	to introduce
la femme	wife/woman	*taquiner	to tease
la fille	daughter/girl	travailler (comme/dans)	to work (as/in)
la grand-mère	grandmother		
une hôtesse de l'air	air hostess	*âgé(e)	old/aged
une infirmière	nurse	*aîné(e)	older
*la jumelle	twin	bon(ne)	good
*les lentilles de contact (pl)	contact lenses	*bouclé(e)	curly
les lunettes (pl)	glasses	*cadet(ette)	younger
la mère	mother	*célibataire	unmarried
*la nièce	niece	châtain(e)	chestnut
*la retraite	retirement	*compréhensif(ive)	understanding
la secrétaire	secretary	*décédé(e)	dead
la sœur	sister	divorcé(e)	divorced
la souris	mouse	*familial(e)	family/ domestic
la tante	aunt	*fier(ière)	proud
la tortue	tortoise	*frisé(e)	curly
		gentil(le)	nice/kind
*agacer	to irritate/annoy	marié(e)	married
s'appeler	to be called	marrant(e)	amusing
*bouleverser	to upset/distress	marron	brown
*énerver	to get on (someone's) nerves	*meilleur(e)	best
		*mignon(ne)	cute
		*reconnaissant(e)	grateful
*se fier à	to trust (in)	*retraité(e)	retired
*gronder	to scold, tell off	sépare(e)	separated
		sérieux(ieuse)	serious (minded)
habiter	to live (in)	unique (fils unique)	only (only son)

1 Self, family and friends

1 Fill in the missing consonants in the following words.

a o _ _ _ e   d _ a _ i

b _ e _ e u   e _ i _ _

c _ e _ _ e

2 Which is the odd word out in the following lists?

a perroquet   cobaye   ouvrier   tortue   souris

b frère   secrétaire   fille   tante   cousin

c infirmière   vendeur   célibataire   chauffeur   hôtesse de l'air

d adulte   copine   sœur   poisson   ami

e anniversaire   amitié   an   nom   animal

3 Definitions. Who is it?

a C'est la mère de mon cousin. _____

b C'est le frère de mon père.   _____

c C'est le père de ma mère.   _____

d C'est le fils de mes parents.   _____

e C'est la fille de ma sœur.   _____

4 Complete the following sentences.

a Mes _____ sont retraités.

b J'ai deux _____ mais je n'ai pas de sœurs.

c J'adore les _____; j'ai deux chiens et un chat.

d Ma mère _____ comme employée de bureau.

e Mes _____ sont divorcés.

5 Anagrams. Write out the word correctly in French. What does it mean in English?

a anipco   b spdnenrtocaro   c nérpmo   d ilmerule   e tletunse

6 Put each of these words in the correct column.

un agent de police   la belle-sœur   le caissier   le chat   le chauffeur
le cheval   la cousine   le demi-frère   le facteur   le lapin   le mari
le poisson rouge   la secrétaire   la souris   la tante

Animal	Travail	Famille

7 Complete the across squares with five pets, and you'll find another one down.

8 Fill in the blanks in this letter using the words below.

anniversaire   ans   appelle   appelle   bonjour

cheveux   frère   mignon   sœur   yeux

_____. Je m'_____ Marie. J'ai 15 _____. Mon
_____ est le 13 mai. J'ai une _____. Elle a les _____
bleus et les _____ chatain. J'ai aussi un _____. Il
s'_____ Antoine. Il est _____.

*les alentours (pl)	surroundings	*le périphérique	ring road
un arbre	tree	*le piéton	pedestrian
un arrêt (d'autobus)	(bus) stop	le port	port
un autobus	bus	*le quartier	district
le bâtiment	building	le soleil	sun
le bord de la mer	seaside	le stationnement	parking
le brouillard	fog	le temps	weather
le bus	bus	le touriste	tourist
le car	coach (bus)	le train	train
le centre-ville	town centre	le trajet	journey
le champ	field	*le vacancier	holiday-maker
le château	castle/stately home	le vent	wind
*le climat	climate	le village	village
le collège	secondary school		

le degré	degree (temperature)	*la banlieue	suburb
*un endroit	place	la bibliothèque	library
*un estivant	summer visitor	la boutique	(small) shop
un habitant	inhabitant	*la brume	mist
l'hôtel de ville	town hall	la campagne	country(side)
le jardin public	park	la cathédrale	cathedral
*le jardin zoologique	zoo	la circulation	traffic
le magasin (le grand magasin)	shop (department store)	la colline	hill
		*une éclaircie	sunny period
		une église	church
le marché	market	la ferme	farm
le métro	underground	la gare	(train) station
le monument	monument	la gare routière	bus station
le musée	museum	la mairie	town hall
*un orage	storm	la mer	sea
*le paysage	scenery	la météo	weather forecast

la neige	snow	il neige	it's snowing
la place	square (in town)	pleuvoir	to rain
la plage	beach	il pleut	it's raining
la pluie	rain	Quel temps fait-il?	What's the weather like?
*les prévisions (pl) (météorologiques)	(weather) forecast	stationner	to park
la rivière	river		
la route	(main) road	beau/belle	fine/nice
la rue	street	*bruyant(e)	noisy
la station	(underground) station	calme	peaceful/calm
		chaud(e)	warm/hot
la température	temperature	*démuni(e)	deprived
la ville	town	ennuyeux(euse)	boring
*la zone piétonne	pedestrian precinct	ensoleillé(e)	sunny
		froid(e)	cold
		historique	historic
avoir chaud	to be hot/warm	industriel(le)	industrial
avoir froid	to be cold	magnifique	magnificent
il fait ...	the weather is ...	mauvais(e)	bad
il fait beau	the weather is fine	maximal(e)	maximum
		moderne	modern
il fait mauvais	the weather is bad	nuageux(euse)	cloudy
		*pauvre	poor
il fait du brouillard	the weather is foggy	pittoresque	picturesque
		*pluvieux(euse)	rainy
il fait du vent	the weather is windy	riche	rich
		souvent	often
il fait du soleil	the weather is sunny	touristique	touristy
		tranquil(le)	quiet
geler	to freeze	vieux (vieille)	old
il gèle	it's freezing		
neiger	to snow		

1 Which is the odd word out in the following lists?

a le touriste   un habitant   le bâtiment   le piéton   un estivant

b le musée   une église   la gare   l'hôtel de ville   le centre-ville

c la route   la rue   la circulation   le soleil   le périphérique

d le temps   un orage   la météo   le trajet   la pluie

2 Write in the vowels to complete these words.

a le   c _ l l _ g _   c les   v _ c _ n c _ _ r s

b la   p l _ c _   d n _ _ g _ _ x

3 Complete this star puzzle.

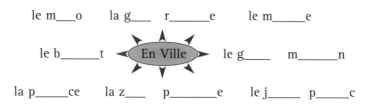

le m___o   la g___   r_____e   le m_____e

le b_____t   En Ville   le g____   m_____n

la p_____ce   la z___   p_____e   le j_____   p_____c

4 Complete the following weather phrases by solving the anagrams.

a Il fait du oliubrldar.   c Il fait uvamisa.

b Il ingee.   d Il tupel.

5 Choose an adjective from this list to complete each blank.

vieille   vieux   industrielle   historique   démuni

a une _____ ville   d un monument _____

b un quartier _____   e un _____ bâtiment

c une grande ville _____

6 Sort the following words into three lists.

le train   le marché   la gare   le château   le musée   la boutique
          le trajet   le jardin zoologique   la station

Magasins	Chemin De Fer	La Ville

7 Fill in the blanks in this poster. Choose the words from the following list.

mer   magasins   ville   musées   boutiques   magnifique
          piétonne   touristes   monuments

Bordeaux est une très grande _____. Dans la
zone _____ il y a beaucoup de _____
et aussi des grands _____. Pour les
_____ il y a des _____ et des
_____. Aux alentours, vous trouverez un
paysage _____. Enfin, la _____ est à
quelques kilomètres.

8 Write the names of

a trois bâtiments qui commencent par la lettre C

b cinq personnes

c cinq choses qu'on trouve à la campagne.

l'allemand	German		le magnétophone	tape recorder
l'anglais	English		le magnétoscope	video recorder
l'art dramatique	drama		le papier	paper
le bac(calauréat)	A-level equivalent		*le programme	syllabus
le bic	biro		*le progrès	progress
le cahier	exercise book		le sac à dos	backpack
le cartable	satchel		le stylo	pen
le collège	(secondary) school		*le surveillant	prefect, supervisor
*le conseiller (d'orientation)	(careers) adviser		le tableau	board
			le taille-crayon	pencil-sharpener
le cours	lesson		le terrain de sport	sports ground
le crayon	pencil		le trimestre	term
le déjeuner	lunch		un uniforme	uniform
le dessin	art			
les devoirs (pl)	homework		la biologie	biology
*le diplôme	diploma		la calculatrice	calculator
le directeur	headteacher		la cantine	dining-hall
un élève	pupil		la chimie	chemistry
un emploi du temps	timetable		une école (primaire)	(primary) school
*l'enseignement	teaching			
l'espagnol	Spanish		l'EMT	craft/CDT
un étudiant	student		l'EPS	PE/games
un examen	examination		la faute	mistake
le français	French		la géographie	geography
le gymnase	gym(nasium)		la gomme	rubber
un instituteur	(primary) teacher		une heure	hour
			l'histoire	history
le laboratoire	laboratory		l'informatique	I.T.
le livre	(text) book		une institutrice	(primary) teacher
le lycée	(sixth form) college		l'instruction civique	civics

l'instruction religieuse	R.E.	étudier	to study
la journée (scolaire)	(school) day	finir	to finish
la langue	language	passer (un examen)	to take (an exam)
la leçon	lesson	poser (une question)	to ask (a question)
les mathématiques (pl) (les maths)	mathematics	préférer	to prefer
la matière	subject	*prêter	to lend
la pause de midi	midday break	barbant(e)	boring
la physique	physics	difficile	difficult
la récréation (récré)	break	en troisième	in Year 10
la règle	ruler	en seconde	in Year 11
la religion	religion	en première	in Year 12
la rentrée	start of school year	facile	easy
*la retenue	detention	*fort(e) (en)	good (at)
*la réunion	meeting	intéressant(e)	interesting
la salle (de classe)	(class) room	*nul(le) (en)	rubbish (at)
les sciences (pl)	science	préféré(e)	favourite
la technologie	technology	sévère	strict
la trousse	pencil case	sympa	nice

aimer	to like
apprendre	to learn
*bavarder	to chat
commencer	to start
copier	to copy
décrire	to describe
dessiner	to draw
détester	to hate
durer	to last
*emprunter	to borrow

1 Complete the across squares with five school subjects, and you'll find another one down.

a C'est une science.

b Langue parlée en France.

c On travaille avec un ordinateur.

d On étudie le passé.

e On fait du sport.

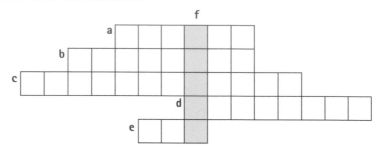

2 Which is the odd one out in the following lists?

a espagnol   allemand   anglais   dessin   français

b directeur   conseiller d'orientation   enseignement   élève   surveillant

c rentrée   faute   trimestre   journée   heure

d cantine   salle de classe   cartable   laboratoire   gymnase

e instruction civique   technologie   devoirs   biologie   EMT

3 Look at the illustrations and fill in the missing words.

Dans la _____ il y a un _____, une _____, une_____, une _____ et un _____.

4 Choose one of the following to complete each sentence.

neuf heures	15h30	10 minutes	une heure

a Les cours commencent à ....

b La pause de midi dure ....

c Il y a une récré de ....

d Les cours finissent à....................

5 Identify these classroom objects and write the missing letters.

a le _ _ _ _ _ _ _ p h o n e   b le _ _ _ _ e a u   c le p _ _ _ _ r

6 Put these words into two lists, positive and negative.

retenue   difficile   nul   fort   sympa   sévère

barbant   intéressant

Positif	Négatif

7 Put an appropriate verb into each sentence.

passe	prêter	bavarder	dessine

a J'aime _____ avec mes copines.

b L'institutrice _____ au tableau.

c Mon frère _____ son baccalauréat.

d Tu peux me _____ un stylo?

un agriculteur	farmer	*le PDG (président-directeur-général)	managing director
*un apprenti	apprentice		
*un apprentissage	apprenticeship	*le pensionnaire	boarder (at school)
*un architecte	architect		
*un artisan	craftsman	le plombier	plumber
l'avenir (à l'avenir)	future (in the future)	le projet	plan
		le (grand) public	(general) public
*un avocat	lawyer	*le racket	extortion
les bijoux (pl)	jewellery	le règlement	rule/regulation
*le boulot	work/job (slang)	le résultat	result
*le cadre	executive	le salaire	salary
le chômage (au chômage)	unemployment (unemployed)	*le syndicat	trade union
		le tourisme	tourism
le chômeur	unemployed person	*le vandalisme	vandalism
le client	customer		
*le commerce	business/trade	les affaires (pl) (de sport)	(sports) gear
*le comptable	accountant	*une agression	attack
*le contrat	contract	la boucle d'oreille	ear-ring
*le droit	(study of) law	la carrière	career
le fonctionnaire	civil servant	*la candidature	application
le gendarme	police officer	*la connaissance	knowledge
*les graffitis (pl)	graffiti	*la discipline	discipline/subject for study
*un homme d'affaires	businessman		
un ingénieur	engineer	(école) de garçons/ de filles	boys'/girls' (school)
*le lycée technique	technical college		
		une équipe	team
le maçon	builder	les études (pl)	studies
*le maquillage	make-up	l'expérience	experience
*le marketing	marketing	*la faculté (la fac)	university
le mécanicien	mechanic		
le métier	job/profession	*la formation (professionnelle)	(professional) training
le patron	boss		

*la licence	(university) degree	(assez) bien	(quite) well
la médecine	medicine	avec	with
la note	mark	chic	smart
la publicité	advertising	content(e)	pleased
*la recherche	research	démodé(e)	outdated
*la responsabilité	responsibility	différent(e)	different
*la sécurité	security/safety	en plein air	in the open air
la terminale	upper sixth	*enrichissant(e)	rewarding
l'université	university	*expérimenté(e)	experienced
la violence	violence	inutile	useless
		mixte	mixed
		payé(e) (bien/mal payé)	paid (well/badly paid)
*s'adresser à	to contact	*polyvalent(e)	versatile
*agresser	to assault	privé(e)	private
attaquer	to attack	professionnel(le)	professional
causer	to cause	public (publique)	public
chercher	to look for	sans	without
continuer	to continue	*satisfaisant	satisfying
écrire	to write	scientifique	scientific
*embaucher	to employ/hire	sûr(e)	safe/secure
encourager	to encourage	utile	useful
envoyer	to send		
gagner	to earn		
*perfectionner	to improve		
protéger	to protect		
rencontrer	to meet		
téléphoner (à)	to telephone		

*à durée déterminée	fixed-term (contract)
à l'étranger	abroad
à la mode	fashionable

1 Complete this grid.

a	apprentie
b	mécanicienne
c	cliente
d	patronne
avocat	e

2 Find the odd one out.

a Which of these words would you not expect to find in a job advert?

cherche   téléphoner   salaire   envoyer   agresser

b Which of these words would you not expect to find in a job application?

candidature   expérience   boucle d'oreille   études   connaissance

3 Put these words into two lists – positive or negative.

chômage   enrichissant   violence   racket   satisfaisant
bien payé   sûr   démodé

Positif	Négatif

4 Fill in the missing letters to find five career opportunities.

a le   m _ r _ e _ i _ g   d le t _ _ r _ _ m _

b la p _ _ l _ _ i _ é   e le c _ _ m _ _ c _

c la _ é _ e _ i _ e

5 Fill in the missing verbs.

| perfectionner | continuer | envoyer | gagner | rencontrer |

a Je vais _____ mes études.

b Je veux _____ le public.

c J'ai l'intention de _____ mon français.

d Je vais vous _____ une lettre.

e Vous n'allez pas _____ un gros salaire.

6 Complete these words. They are things that may not be allowed at school!

a le r _ _ _ _ _

b le m _ _ _ _ _ _ _ _ _

c les b _ _ _ _ _

d le v _ _ _ _ _ _ _ _

e les g _ _ _ _ _ _ _

7 Definitions. Who is it?

a Il construit les maisons.

b Il répare les automobiles.

c Elle dessine les maisons.

d Il n'a pas d'emploi.

e Il travaille à la ferme.

8 Find the profession by solving the anagrams.

a eginnérui   d plombtacc

b molperbi   e endgamer

c refactnoinino

un aéroglisseur	hovercraft	*les transports (pl) en commun	public transport
un aéroport	airport	le tunnel	tunnel
un aller-retour	return ticket	le vélo	bike
un aller simple	single	le vélomoteur	moped
un avion	plane	le vol	flight
les bagages (pl)	luggage	le voyageur	passenger
le bateau	boat	*le wagon-lit	sleeping-car
le billet	ticket	*le wagon-restaurant	restaurant-car
le buffet	refreshment room		
le carnet	book of tickets	une agence de voyages	travel agent's
le chemin de fer	railway	*une aire de repos	motorway services
le départ	departure		
*l'embarquement	boarding	l'arrivée	arrival
un express	slow train	une auto	car
les feux (pl) (rouges)	traffic lights	une autoroute (la A6)	motorway (the M6)
le gazole	diesel		
le guichet	ticket office	*la bagnole	car (slang)
*un hélicoptère	helicopter	la bicyclette	bicycle
un horaire	timetable	la carte	map
le parking	car park	*la ceinture de sécurité	seat-belt
le quai	platform		
le rapide	express	la circulation	traffic
les renseignements (pl)	information	la consigne (automatique)	left luggage (locker)
le retard	delay	la correspondance	connection
*le supplément	extra charge	*la couchette	bed (on train)
*le TGV	high speed train	l'essence	petrol
le taxi	taxi	la gare	(train) station
le ticket	ticket (bus, métro)	la gare routière	bus station

la ligne	line/route (buses)	descendre de	to get off
la moto	motorbike	faire le plein	to fill up (with petrol)
la piste	runway	il faut	(you) have to
la place	seat	manquer	to miss
la porte	(departure) gate (at airport)	monter dans	to get on
la portière	door (of car/ bus/train etc)	partir	to leave
la réservation	reservation	prendre	to catch
la route nationale	main (A) road	réserver	to book
la salle d'attente	waiting room	rouler (à 130km/h)	to travel (at 80 mph)
la SNCF	French railways	tomber en panne	to break down
la sortie (No6)	motorway junction (No6)	voyager	to travel
*la sortie de secours	emergency exit	à destination de	going to (by train/plane)
la station (de métro)	(underground) station	direct(e)	direct/non-stop
la station-service	petrol station	*direction ...	in the direction of
la traversée	crossing	en (voiture, etc)	by (car, etc)
la voie	track	en provenance de	coming from (by train/ plane)
la voiture	car	(non-)fumeur	(non-)smoking
annoncer	to announce	*immédiat(e)	immediate
attendre	to wait	première/deuxième classe	first/second class
*atterrir	to land (plane)	prochain(e)	next
arriver	to arrive	sans plomb	lead free
*avoir le regret	to regret	votre attention, s'il vous plaît	your attention please
changer	to change		
composter	to punch (ticket)		
*décoller	to take off (plane)		

1 Which is the odd word out in the following lists?

a voiture   auto   taxi   carte   bagnole

b rapide   TGV   express   train   renseignements

c vélo   avion   moto   vélomoteur   bicyclette

d quai   feux rouges   buffet   guichet   consigne

e aéroglisseur   bateau   circulation   hélicoptère   vélo

f aller-retour   bicyclette   ticket   carnet   aller simple

2 Complete the following places connected with travel.

a l' _ _ _ _ port

b la _ _ _ _ routière

c la _ _ _ _ _ _ _ de métro

d une _ _ _ _ de repos

e une _ _ _ _ _ _ de voyages

3 Put these words and phrases in the appropriate columns.

composter votre billet   deuxième classe   essence   faire le plein
gazole   piste   porte No8   sans plomb   SNCF   vol AF218

Gare	Aéroport	Station-service

4 Solve the clues.

a En voiture, il faut mettre la _ _ _ _ _ _ _ _ _ _ _ _ _ _ _ _ _.

b Sur l' _ _ _ _ _ _ _ _ _ on peut rouler à 130km/h.

c On laisse les bagages à la _ _ _ _ _ _ _ _.

d Ce train est _ _ _ _ _ _. Il ne faut pas changer.

e C'est l'autoroute A10, _ _ _ _ _ _ No 13.

5 Find the opposites to complete the table.

à destination de	**a**
b	arrivée
aller simple	**c**
d	descendre de
atterrir	**e**

6 Find a French word to fit each of the clues.

a Lots of cars, lorries etc.

b To book a seat in advance.

c Where you can eat on a train.

d Getting off one train to catch another.

e A higher price you have to pay on some trains.

7 Solve the clues and find five kinds of transport.

a This crosses the water.

b So does this, on a cushion of air.

c This shows you how to get there.

d This has a big propeller – on top!

e Boeing, Lockheed, Concorde.

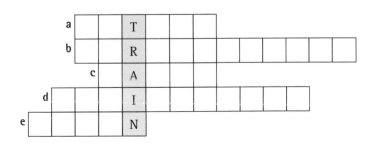

le carrefour	crossroads
le cinéma	cinema
le coin	corner
le commissariat	police station
les feux (pl) (rouges)	traffic lights
le fleuve	river
un hôtel	hotel
le palais	palace
le plan (de la ville)	(town) plan
le pont	bridge
le rond-point	roundabout

la banque	bank
la bibliothèque	library
la cabine téléphonique	phone box
la pharmacie	chemist's
la rue	street
les toilettes (pl)	toilets

aller	to go
continuer	to continue
être situé(e)	to be (situated)
faire demi-tour	to turn back
il y a	there is
prendre	to take
tourner	to turn
traverser	to cross
se trouver	to be (situated)

à côté de	next to
à droite	(on the) right

la première à droite	first right
à gauche	(on the) left
la deuxième à gauche	second left
à (cent) mètres	(100) metres away
à pied	on foot
à sens unique	one way
après	after
avant	before
derrière	behind
devant	in front of/ outside

en face de	opposite
entre ... et ...	between ... and ...

Excusez-moi	Excuse me
jusqu'à	as far as
juste	just
(C'est) loin (?)	(Is it) far (?)
Où se trouve ...	where is ...
Pardon	Excuse me
Pour aller à ...	How do I get to ...
près d'ici	nearby
tout droit	straight on

Allez ...	Go ...
Continuez ...	Carry on ...
Passez ...	Pass ...
Prenez ...	Take ...
Tournez ...	Turn ...
Traversez ...	Cross ...

1 In each sentence, replace the symbols with the appropriate French words or phrases.

i   ii   iii   iv   v   vi   vii

a Aux .... tournez à ....

c Tournez à .... au ....

b Prenez la ....

d Continuez .... et traversez le ....

2 Look at this picture, then complete the sentences.

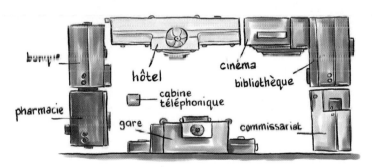

banque hôtel cinéma bibliothèque cabine téléphonique pharmacie gare commissariat

a La bibliothèque est _ _ _ _ _ _ _ _ la banque.

b Le commissariat est _ _ _ _ _ _ _ la bibliothèque.

c L'hôtel est _ _ _ _ _ le cinéma et la banque.

d Il y a une cabine téléphonique _ _ _ _ _ _ la pharmacie.

3 Find the opposites to complete the table.

devant	**a**
b	après
près d'ici	**c**
à droite	**d**

l'accueil	reception	les sports (pl) (d'hiver/ nautiques)	sports (winter/ water)
*l'alpinisme	mountaineering		
un appareil photo	camera	le syndicat d'initiative	tourist office
l'après-midi	afternoon		
l'automne	autumn	*le terrain de jeux	playground
le ballon (de foot)	(foot) ball	le tour (du monde)	(world) tour
*le caméscope	video-camera	*le voyage organisé	package holiday
*le cirque	circus		
le club (Mickey)	(beach) club (for children)	une activité	activity
		la balle (de tennis)	(tennis) ball
le dépliant	leaflet	la brochure	brochure
l'été	summer	la campagne	country(side)
*le feu d'artifice	firework display	*la chaleur	heat
le groupe	group	*la classe de neige	winter-sports school
l'hiver	winter		
le lac	lake	la colonie de vacances	children's holiday camp
*le maître-nageur	life-guard		
le matin	morning	la côte	coast
*le moniteur	instructor	la crème (solaire)	(sun) cream
un office de tourisme	tourist office	la distraction	entertainment
		une entrée	admission/ entrance
le parc	park		
le paysage	scenery	une excursion	excursion/trip
le pique-nique	picnic	*la grotte	cave/grotto
le printemps	spring	les heures (pl) (d'ouverture)	(opening) times
*le scooter de mer	jet-ski		
le séjour	stay	la liste	list
*le site (touristique)	(tourist) attraction	les lunettes de soleil (pl)	sunglasses
*le ski nautique	water-skiing	la montagne	mountain
le soir	evening	la nuit	night
le spectacle	show	les palmes (pl)	flippers

la pellicule	film (for camera)	à partir de	from (prices/ times)
la photo(graphie)	photo(graph)	compris(e)	included
la planche (à voile)	wind-surfing, wind-surf board	de ... à ...	from (time) to (time)
*la plongée (sous-marine)	diving (under the sea)	du ... au ...	from (date) to (date)
*la randonnée	walking/ rambling	*en pleine saison	at the height of the season
la saison	season	fermé(e)	closed
la tour (Eiffel)	(Eiffel) tower	gratuit(e)	free (of charge)
la valise	(suit) case	guidé(e)	guided
la vallée	valley	moins de (10 ans)	under/ less than (10)
la visite	visit	ouvert(e) (de ... à)	open (from ... to)
la vue	view	*payant(e)	to be paid for
		son et lumière	sound and light
se baigner	to bathe/go in the water	toute l'année	all the year round
bronzer	to tan/go brown	toutes les demi- heures/vingt minutes	every half-hour/ twenty minutes
défaire ses valises	to unpack		
faire ses bagages	to pack		
louer	to hire		
prendre un bain de soleil	to sunbathe		
*supporter (je ne supporte pas la chaleur)	to stand (I can't stand the heat)		
visiter	to visit		

(non) accompagné	(un) accompanied
*(pas) admis	(not) admitted

1 Find the opposites and complete the table.

gratuit	a
b	fermé
matin	c
été	d

2 Put the following activities in the appropriate column.

alpinisme   photographie   ski   scooter   sports d'hiver
ski nautique   plongée sous-marine   excursion   planche à voile

Au bord de la mer	En montagne	Mer ou montagne

3 Which is the odd word out in the following lists?

a nuit   lunettes de soleil   palmes   crème solaire   pellicule

b vallée   côte   lac   grotte   après-midi

c cirque   site touristique   feu d'artifice   balle   grotte

d accueil   syndicat d'initiative   parc   office de tourisme
agence de voyages

e printemps   été   soir   automne   hiver

4 Fill in the missing vowels to find five things you might do on holiday.

a p _ q _ _ - n _ q _ _   **d** _ x c _ r s _ _ n

b v _ s _ t _   **e** _ l p _ n _ s m _

c b _ _ n d _ s _ l _ _ l

5 Find the French words for the following in this wordsearch.

rambling   admission   tower   to tan   scenery   coast

group   video-camera   stay   water- (le ski ....)   heat

R	A	N	D	O	N	N	E	E
C	P	A	Y	S	A	G	E	T
C	H	A	L	E	U	R	N	O
O	Z	U	I	J	T	O	T	U
T	W	U	J	O	I	U	R	R
E	S	K	D	U	Q	P	E	A
G	H	N	X	R	U	E	E	M
B	R	O	N	Z	E	R	Q	R
C	A	M	E	S	C	O	P	E

6 Look at this advert for a local cave, then complete the English sentences.

GROTTE DU LOUP

ouverte toute l'année

entrée **65F**/10 euros
(gratuite pour les moins de 12 ans
accompagnés d'un adulte)

les chiens ne sont pas admis

visites guidées toutes les demi-heures

---

a The cave is open ....

b Children under 12 do not have to .... if they are
....

c Dogs are not ....

d There is a guided tour every ....

le balcon	balcony
le bar	bar
le bloc sanitaire	shower block
le camping	campsite
*le confort	comfort
le déjeuner	lunch
le dentifrice	toothpaste
le dîner	evening meal
le dortoir	dormitory
le drap	sheet
un emplacement	site (on a campsite)
le gaz	gas
un gîte	holiday home
un hôtel	hotel
le (grand) lit	(double) bed
*le luxe	luxury
*le matelas	mattress
*le matériel (de camping)	(camping) equipment
le mois (de juin)	month (of June)
un ouvre-boîte	can-opener
un ouvre-bouteille	bottle-opener
le passeport	passport
le petit déjeuner	breakfast
*le piquet	tent-peg
*le poêle	stove
le réceptionniste	receptionist
le robinet	tap
le sac de couchage	sleeping bag
le savon	soap

le tarif	price-list
le téléphone	telephone
*le tire-bouchon	corkscrew

une alimentation	food-shop
*l'animation	entertainment
*des arrhes	deposit
une auberge de jeunesse	youth hostel
la brosse à dents	toothbrush
la caravane	caravan
la carte	card
*la caution	breakage deposit
la chambre	(bed)room
la chambre de famille	family room
double	double (room)
*la chambre d'hôte	bed and breakfast
la clé	key
la couverture	blanket
la demi-pension	half-board
la douche	shower
l'eau (chaude/froide)	(hot/cold) water
une étoile	star
la fiche	form
la glace	ice
la lampe (de poche)	(pocket) torch
la location	hire
la note	bill (at hotel)
la pension complète	full-board

la pièce d'identité	ID	animé(e)	lively/with entertainment
la place	space, room	bon marché	cheap
*les plats cuisinés à emporter	take-away meals	*chauffé(e)	heated
la poubelle	dustbin	(pas) cher (chère)	(not) expensive
*la prise (de courant)	power point	complet (complète)	full (up)
la réception	reception	*gonflable	inflatable
la réservation	reservation	libre	vacant, free
la salle de jeux	games room	*ombragé(e)	shady
la serviette	towel	par écrit	in writing
la tente	tent	par nuit	per night
		par personne	per person
confirmer	to confirm	(non) potable	(not) drinking water
descendre dans (un hôtel)	to stay in (a hotel)	pour ... nuit(s)	for ... nights
dormir	to sleep	pour ... personne(s)	for ... people
faire la cuisine	to cook	*(quatre) étoiles	(four) star (restaurant/hotel)
faire du camping	to go camping		
fermer	to close	sale	dirty
fonctionner	to work	*vers (...h)	about (... o'clock)
garer	to park		
*gonfler	to blow up (inflate)		
marcher	to work		
répondre	to reply		
rester	to stay		
réveiller	to wake up		
servir	to serve		
*verser (des arrhes)	to pay (a deposit)		

1 Where shall we stay? Look at the following definitions.

a Maison qu'on loue, généralement à la campagne.

b Logement pour les jeunes – pas cher!

c Terrain pour les tentes et les caravanes.

d On descend ici si on veut le confort.

2 Complete these articles you would need on a camping holiday.

a l _ m p _ d _ p _ c h _

b p _ _ l _

c m _ t _ l _ s

d _ _ v r _ - b _ _ t _

e t _ n t _

3 Put the following in the appropriate columns.

bloc sanitaire   chambre de famille   demi-pension   gaz
grand lit   piquet   sac de couchage

Hôtel	Camping

4 Find five words which end in ...tion. What do they mean?

5 What is it ? Find the French word or phrase which fits each of these definitions.

  a Somewhere to plug in your electrical equipment.

  b Document to prove your identity – a passport or a driving licence, for example.

  c All the things you need to go camping.

  d A stay at a hotel which includes all your meals.

6 Which is the odd word/phrase out in each of these lists?

  a chambre d'hôte   gîte   passeport   auberge de jeunesse   hôtel

  b arrhes   caution   note   tire-bouchon   tarif

  c quatre étoiles   sale   ombragé   de luxe   tout confort

  d savon   serviette   poêle   brosse à dents   dentifrice

7 You receive a letter from a campsite. Some of the words are unclear. What are they?

  a Notre tarif est de 65F/10 euros par p............................. par nuit.

  b La l.............................. de sacs de c............................. est possible à l'accueil.

  c Il y a une piscine ch............................. .

  d Le camping est très a.............................é.

  e Veuillez c............................. votre réservation par é............................. .

8 Find the missing verb(s) in each sentence.

  a Ma mère veut d................... dans un hôtel, car elle n'aime pas .... la cuisine.

  b Où est-ce que je peux g................... ma voiture ?

  c Voulez-vous me r................... à huit heures ?

  d L'eau chaude ne m................... pas.

le Canada	Canada	*le premier ministre	Prime Minister
le Danemark	Denmark	le président	president
les Etats-Unis (pl)	United States		
*le Japon	Japan	*l'Afrique	Africa
*le Maroc	Morocco	l'Allemagne	Germany
*le Massif Central	Central mountain range in France	les Alpes (pl)	Alps
		l'Amérique	America
		l'Angleterre	England
le Midi	South of France	l'Autriche	Austria
les Pays-Bas (pl)	Netherlands	la Belgique	Belgium
le pays de Galles	Wales	la Bretagne	Brittany (region)
le Portugal	Portugal		
*le Québec	Quebec (French -speaking area of Canada)	l'Ecosse	Scotland
		l'Espagne	Spain
		l'Europe	Europe
le Rhin	(river) Rhine	la France	France
le Rhône	(river) Rhône	la Grande-Bretagne	Great Britain
le roi	king	la Grèce	Greece
le Royaume-Uni	United Kingdom	la Hollande	Holland
		l'Irlande (du Nord)	(Northern) Ireland
*le conseil municipal	town council		
*le continent	continent	l'Italie	Italy
le département	French equivalent of English county	la Manche	(English) Channel
		la Méditerranée	Mediterranean
le douanier	customs officer	la Normandie	Normandy (region)
un étranger	foreigner		
*le gouvernement	government	la reine	queen
un habitant	inhabitant	*la Russie	Russia
*un indigène	native	*la Suède	Sweden
le monde	world	la Suisse	Switzerland
*un océan	ocean	*la communauté	community
le pays	country	*la commune	district/village

la douane	customs	italien(ne)[1]	Italian
la frontière	frontier	japonais(e)[1]	Japanese
la langue	language	portugais(e)[1]	Portuguese
la nationalité	nationality	russe[1]	Russian
la population	population	suédois(e)[1]	Swedish
les Pyrénées (pl)	Pyrenees	suisse	Swiss
la région	region		
l'UE	European Union	à l'étranger	abroad
		au	in (+ masculine countries)
africain(e)	African		
allemand(e)[1]	German	aux	in (+ plural countries)
américain(e)	American		
anglais(e)[1]	English	en	in (+ feminine countries)
autrichien(ne)	Austrian		
belge	Belgian	*bilingue	bilingual
britannique	British	*international(e)	international
canadien(ne)	Canadian	*natal(e)	native
danois(e)[1]	Danish	(le pays natal de X)	(X's native country)
écossais(e)	Scottish		
espagnol(e)[1]	Spanish	national(e)	national
européen(ne)	European	régional(e)	regional
flamand(e)[1]	Flemish (language spoken in Belgium)	Bruxelles	Brussels
		Douvres	Dover
		Edimbourg	Edinburgh
français(e)[1]	French	Londres	London
*francophone	French-speaking	Marseille	Marseilles
gallois(e)[1]	Welsh		
grec(que)[1]	Greek		
hollandais(e)[1]	Dutch		
indien(ne)	Indian		
irlandais(e)[1]	Irish		

[1 The masculine form of these adjectives is also used for the language]

1 Match the language with the country.

   a hollandais   **b** gallois   **c** flamand   **d** anglais   **e** français

   Belgique   Etats-Unis   Pays-Bas   Suisse   pays de Galles

2 Which is the odd one out in the following lists?

   a l'Allemagne   la Suède   le Danemark   le Canada   la Grèce

   b les Alpes   le Rhin   le Rhône   la Méditerranée   la Manche

   c le Midi   la Bretagne   la Normandie   le Québec   le Massif Central

   d le douanier   le président   la région   le premier ministre   l'étranger

   e le Maroc   le Canada   la Suisse   l'Angleterre   la Belgique

3 Complete the following grid.

autrichien	autrichienne
écossais	**a**
b	indienne
canadien	**c**
d	belge

4 Match the flag with the country.

a

b

c

d

e

f

Italie   Etats-Unis   Japon   Grande-Bretagne   Allemagne   France

5 Find the missing word in each of the following sentences.

> nationalité   natal   francophone   bilingue   président   population

a La .... de l'Union Européenne est de 250 million d'habitants.

b En Angleterre, il y a une reine; en France, il y a un ....

c Le Maroc est un pays ....

d Thierry Henri est de .... française.

e Le pays .... d'Hercule Poirot, c'est la Belgique.

f Une personne qui parle italien et grec est ....

6 Put the following words in the correct column in the grid.

Irlande du Nord   Québec   Normandie   Espagne   Marseille   Londres

Japon   Russie   Rhône   Portugal   Ecosse   Autriche   Midi   Bruxelles

Le Royaume-Uni	La France	L'Union européenne	Le Monde

7 Find the missing words in each of the following sentences.

a Il est né au Danemark; il est ....

b Elle est née en Italie; elle est ....

c Il est né à Edimbourg; il est ....

d Elle est née à Douvres; elle est ....

e Il est né à Madrid; il est ....

*un appel	(phone) call	le permis de conduire	driving licence
l'argent	money	*le phare	headlamp
le billet (de ... francs/euros)	(... francs/euros) note	le pneu	tyre
*le bracelet	bracelet	*le portable	mobile phone
le bureau de change	exchange bureau	le portefeuille	wallet
le bureau des objets trouvés	lost property office	le porte-monnaie	purse
le carnet de chèques	cheque book	*le poste (de police)	(police) station
le chèque (de voyage)	(traveller's) cheque	le radiateur	radiator
*le chéquier	cheque book	le sac (à main)	(hand) bag
le code postal	post code	le timbre (poste)	(postage) stamp
*le colis	parcel	un timbre à ... francs/euros	a ... franc/euro stamp
*le contenu	contents	le volant	steering wheel
le distributeur de billets	cash machine (hole in wall)		
l'euro	euro (currency)	la bague	ring
le formulaire	form	la banque	bank
le franc	franc	la batterie	battery (in car)
le frein	brake	la boîte aux lettres	letter box
*GDF (Gaz de France)	gas company	la caisse	cash desk
le garage	garage	la carte de crédit	credit card
le guichet	window (e.g. in bank)	la carte (postale)	(post) card
*l'indicatif	dialling code	*la crevaison	puncture
le moteur	engine	*EDF (Electricité de France)	Electricity company
le numéro (*d'immatriculation)	number (registration)	France Télécom	Telephone company
le paquet	parcel	l'huile	oil
le parapluie	umbrella	la lettre	letter
*le pare-brise	windscreen	la livre (sterling)	pound (sterling)
		*la levée	collection (from letter box)
		la marque	make/brand
		la montre	watch

la pièce (de ... francs/euros)	(... franc/euro) coin	téléphoner	to telephone
la poste	post office	tomber en panne	to break down
la roue	wheel	*toucher	to cash (a cheque)
la signature	signature		
la télécarte	phone card	Allô	Hello (on telephone)
la tonalité	(dialling) tone	C'est le garage X?	Is that X garage?
la valeur	value		
		crevé(e)	punctured
aider	to help	dedans	inside
attendre	to wait (for)	*dessus	on (it)
changer	to change	en argent	(made of) silver
composer	to dial	en cuir	(made of) leather
*contenir	to contain		
décrire	to describe	en espèces	in cash
*décrocher	to lift the receiver	en or	(made of) gold
		en panne	out of order
dépanner	to fix/repair	Il/Elle est de quelle couleur/ marque?	What colour/ make is it?
envoyer	to send		
introduire	to insert	*immatriculé(e)	registered (car no)
introduisez une pièce	insert a coin		
		le/la/l'/les	it/them
laisser	to leave (behind)	Où/Quand l'avez vous perdu(e)?	Where/When did you lose it?
perdre	to lose		
raccrocher	to hang up	Pouvez-vous le/la/les décrire?	Can you describe it/ them?
remplir	to fill in/ complete		
		Pouvez-vous m'aider?	Can you help me?
réparer	to repair		
*faire réparer	to have repaired	*recommandé(e)	registered (letter)
retirer	to take out/ withdraw		
signer	to sign		

1 Match up the halves of these sentences.

a Ma voiture est ...

b J'ai perdu une ...

c Vous devez composer ...

d Je voudrais envoyer ...

e Je voudrais changer ...

i ... le numéro.

ii ... un colis en Angleterre.

iii ... tombée en panne.

iv ... dix livres sterling.

v ... bague en or.

2 Find the French word or phrase to solve these clues.

a You can get money at any time here.

b You carry change in it.

c The car lights won't work without it.

d You have to fill this in at the lost property office.

e You can make a phone call from anywhere with this.

3 Put these words into the correct column.

timbre   chèque   télécarte   code postal   indicatif   billet de 100F/euros
livre sterling   paquet   portable   lettre

La Banque	La Poste	France Télécom

4 Find the odd word out in each of the following lists.

a euro   billet   timbre   pièce   franc

b pneu   phare   appel   pare-brise   roue

c billet   chèque de voyage   volant   carte de crédit   pièce

d téléphoner   toucher   raccrocher   décrocher   composer

5 Complete the crossword with five items of lost property, and you will find a sixth item.

  a You wear it on your wrist.

  b It stops you getting wet.

  c It tells the time.

  d You have to go to the Post Office to send this.

  e You need it to write a cheque.

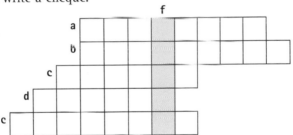

6 Fill in the missing words in these sentences.

portefeuille   signer   numéro   espèces   crevé

  a Je vais payer en ....

  b J'ai un pneu ....

  c Voulez-vous .... ici?

  d Quel est votre .... de téléphone?.

  e J'ai perdu mon ....

7 Solve these anagrams. They are all words you might need when filling in a lost property form.

  a isslaer   **d** tnocnue

  b grenat   **e** drupe

  c ricu

un accident (de la route)	(road) accident	*le poignet	wrist
*le bleu	bruise	*le remède	remedy
le bras	arm	le rendez-vous	appointment
*le centre hospitalier	(general) hospital	le rhume	cold
le cœur	heart	*le SAMU	ambulance service
le comprimé	tablet	le sang	blood
le corps	body	le (sapeur-) pompier	fireman
le cou	neck	le sirop	(liquid) medicine
*le coude	elbow	le sparadrap	(sticking) plaster
le dentiste	dentist		
le docteur	doctor	le ventre	stomach
le doigt	finger	les yeux (pl)	eyes
le dos	back		
l'estomac	stomach	une ambulance	ambulance
le genou	knee	*la blessure	wound/injury
un hôpital	hospital	la bouche	mouth
le mal (mal de tête) (mal de mer) (mal aux dents)	pain (headache) (sea-sickness) (toothache)	*la cheville	ankle
		la crise cardiaque	heart attack
		la dent	tooth
le malade	patient	*une entorse	sprain
le médicament	medicine	une épaule	shoulder
le médecin	doctor	la fièvre	temperature/ fever
le nez	nose		
l'œil	eye	la gorge	throat
*un orteil	toe	la grippe	flu
*un os	bone	la jambe	leg
le pharmacien	chemist	la main	hand
le pied	foot	la maladie	illness
*le plâtre	plaster (of Paris)	la mort	death
		une ordonnance	prescription

une oreille	ear	garder le lit	to stay in bed
*la pastille	pastille	*guérir	to cure
*la pilule	pill	*hospitaliser	to send to hospital
la piqûre	sting/bite	piquer	to sting, bite
la piqûre	injection	prendre	to take
la police	police	se reposer	to rest
la radio	X-ray	tomber malade	to fall ill
la santé	health	tousser	to cough
la tête	head	transporter	to take (transport)
*la toux	cough	vomir	to be sick
la trousse de premiers secours	first-aid kit		
*les urgences (pl)	emergency (ward) casualty	Au secours!	Help!
		avant/après les repas	before/after meals
*la victime	victim	blessé(e)	wounded/ injured
		*commotionné(e)	concussed
aller mieux	to get/feel better	(deux/trois) fois par jour	(two/three) times a day
appeler	to call	*d'urgence	urgently/as an emergency
avoir mal à (l'oreille)	to have a pain in (the ear) (= earache)	enrhumé(e)	suffering from a cold
avoir mal au cœur	to feel sick	grave	serious
(se) blesser	to injure (oneself)	malade	ill
se casser (le bras)	to break (one's arm)	sain(e)	healthy
se couper (le doigt)	to cut (one's finger)		
dormir	to sleep		
se faire mal à (la jambe)	to hurt one's (leg)		

1 Find the French for these parts of the body in the wordsearch.

ankle
wrist
body
arm
eye
heart
mouth
neck
nose
stomach

G	S	C	O	U	V	R	W
F	O	E	I	L	H	D	L
C	H	E	V	I	L	L	E
R	C	O	E	U	R	N	B
B	O	U	C	H	E	E	C
B	R	A	S	Y	Q	Z	E
M	P	O	I	G	N	E	T
E	S	T	O	M	A	C	A

2 Complete these sentences with the appropriate word from this list.

ordonnance   pieds   hôpital   tête   comprimé

a Mes chaussures sont trop petites. J'ai mal aux ....

b Je vais prendre de l'aspirine. J'ai mal à la ....

c Le médecin m'a donné une ....

d Je dois prendre un .... trois fois par jour.

e Je vais à l'.................... en ambulance.

3 Which of the following might be involved in a car accident?

pharmacien   toux   sang   dentiste   centre hospitalier

radio   police   blessure   pompier   SAMU

4 Solve the anagrams to find five things you would get from the chemist's.

a dapspraar   b émicdatenm   c spalelit   d poirs   e luplie

5 Where would you go for help with the following?

rhume jambe cassée mal de mer fièvre crise cardiaque grippe

Médecin	Hôpital

6 Find the French word for these definitions.

a Keep one in the car in case of accidents.

b The doctor – or a wasp – might give you this!

c Most people have ten of these.

d You could do this to your wrist or ankle.

e You go to the dentist with this problem.

7 Which is the odd word out in these lists?

a pompier pharmacien docteur remède dentiste

b toux fièvre crise cardiaque rhume mal à la gorge

c coude bras main poignet orteil

d malade enrhumé blessé commotionné mort

un appartement	flat	un ordinateur	computer
un arbre	tree	le placard	cupboard
le buffet	sideboard	*le plafond	ceiling
le bureau	desk	le plancher	floor
le canapé	settee	le premier étage	first floor
le chauffage central	central heating	le poster	poster
le congélateur	freezer	le quartier	district
*un escabeau	step-ladder	le réveil	alarm clock
un escalier	stairs	le rez-de-chaussée	ground floor
l'étage	floor/storey	le rideau	curtain
le premier étage	first floor	*le robinet	tap
le deuxième étage	second floor	le salon	living-room
*un évier	sink	le tapis	carpet
le fauteuil	armchair	le téléphone	telephone
*le four	oven	*le téléviseur	TV set
*le four à	microwave	le toit	roof
micro-ondes	oven	le vestibule	hall
le frigo	fridge	les WC (pl)	toilet
le garage	garage		
*le gazon	lawn	une adresse	address
le grenier	loft	les affaires	things/
un immeuble	block of flats		belongings
le jardin (potager)	(vegetable)	*une antenne	aerial
	garden	une antenne	satellite dish
le jardinage	gardening	parabolique	
le lavabo	washbasin	une armoire	wardrobe
le lave-linge	washing	la baignoire	bath
	machine	la cave	cellar
le lave-vaisselle	dishwasher	la chaîne-stéréo/	stereo
le lit	bed	hi-fi	
le meuble	furniture	la chaise	chair
le miroir	mirror	la chambre	bedroom
le mur	wall		

la chambre d'amis	spare room	décorer	to decorate
la cheminée	chimney/fire-place	*déménager	to move (house)
la clé	key	donner sur	to look out onto
la cuisine	kitchen	habiter	to live (in)
la cuisinière (à gaz/électrique)	cooker (gas/electric)	partager	to share
la douche	shower	au-dessus de	above
*une échelle	ladder	confortable	comfortable
la fenêtre	window	en brique	(made of) brick
la fleur	flower	en pierre	(made of) stone
*une HLM	council house/flat	grand(e)	big
la lampe	lamp	*jumelé(e)	semi-detached
la machine à coudre	sewing machine	meublé(e)	furnished
la maison	house	moderne	modern
*la moquette	fitted carpet	petit(e)	small
la pelouse	lawn	vieux (vieille)	old
la pièce	room		
la plante	plant		
la porte (la porte d'entrée)	door (front door)		
la route	(main) road		
la salle à manger	dining-room		
la salle de bains	bathroom		
la salle de séjour	sitting-room		
la table	table		
la terrasse	terrace/patio		
les toilettes (pl)	toilets		
*la villa	villa		
la vue	view		

1 Complete the labels for this house.

a le   _ _ e _ i e _

b le   _ e u _ i è _ e   é _ a _ e

c le   _ _ e _ i e _   é _ a _ e

d le   _ e _ - _ e - _ _ a u _ _ é e

e la   _ a _ e

2 Which is the odd word out in the following lists?

a mur   toit   plancher   plafond   rideau

b maison   échelle   appartement   HLM   immeuble

c moderne   petit   confortable   terrasse   vieux

d moquette   pelouse   jardin   arbre   fleur

e chambre   cuisine   salle à manger   fenêtre   salon

3 Put the following in the right rooms.

four   fauteuil   canapé   lave-vaisselle   téléviseur   baignoire
cuisinière   douche   congélateur   lavabo

Cuisine	Salle de bains	Salon

4 Find the French words to fit these definitions.

  a You keep the car there.

  b It's for washing clothes.

  c You use it to get to the first floor.

  d You sit round it to keep warm.

  e It should wake you up in the morning.

5 Fill in the missing vowels to find five things you might find in a house.

  a t _ p _ s

  b _ s c _ b _ _ _

  c m _ r _ _ r

  d v _ s t _ b _ l _

  e t _ _ l _ t t _ s

6 Complete these sentences with the missing verb.

habite	décorer	donne	déménage	partage

  a Je veux .... ma chambre en bleu et blanc.

  b Je .... ma chambre avec mon frère.

  c Elle .... dans une nouvelle maison.

  d J' .... une maison en pierre.

  e Ma chambre .... sur un grand jardin.

7 Solve these clues.

  a On y trouve des plantes et des arbres.

  b Il en faut une pour avoir la télévision par satellite.

  c On y fait la vaisselle (si on n'a pas de lave-vaisselle!)

  d Il en faut une pour ouvrir la porte.

l'argent de poche	pocket money	se brosser	to brush
un aspirateur	vacuum cleaner	(les dents)	(one's teeth)
le déjeuner	lunch	(les cheveux)	(one's hair)
le dîner	evening meal/ dinner	se coucher	to go to bed
le fer à repasser	iron	débarrasser la table	to clear the table
le goûter	tea (snack)	demander	to ask
le jardinage	gardening	(à quelqu'un)	(someone)
le ménage	housework	(de faire quelque chose)	(to do something)
*les ordures (pl)	rubbish	se déshabiller	to get undressed
*le peigne	comb	devoir	to have to
le rasoir	razor	donner	to give
le repas (du soir)	(evening) meal	essuyer (la vaisselle)	to dry (the dishes)
le repassage	ironing	faire	to do
		(faire la cuisine)	(to do the cooking)
les affaires (pl)	things/ belongings	(faire les courses)	(to do the shopping)
la brosse	brush	(faire le repassage)	(to do the ironing)
les courses (pl)	shopping	(faire les devoirs)	(to do homework)
la cuisine	the cooking	(faire du baby-sitting)	(to baby-sit)
la lessive	washing	(faire du jardinage)	(to do some gardening)
la poubelle	dustbin	(faire la vaisselle)	(to do the washing-up)
*la tondeuse	lawn-mower	faire	to make
la vaisselle	washing-up	(faire le lit)	(to make the bed)
aider (quelqu'un)	to help (someone)	faire la grasse matinée	to have a lie-in
(à faire quelque chose)	(to do something)	il (me) faut	(I) have to
aller au lit	to go to bed	gagner	to earn
*arroser (les plantes)	to water (the plants)		

s'habiller	to get dressed	à ... heures	at ... o'clock
laver (la voiture)	to wash (the car)	à ... heures (dix)	at (ten) past...
se laver	to have a wash	à ... heures moins (vingt)	at (twenty) to ...
se lever	to get up	après	after
mettre la table	to set the table	avant	before
nettoyer	to clean	de temps en temps	from time to time
passer l'aspirateur	to vacuum		
*se peigner	to comb one's hair	d'habitude	usually
		*en désordre	in a mess
prendre (une douche) (un bain)	to have (a shower) (a bath)	en semaine	on a weekday
		le dimanche	on Sundays
		le samedi	on Saturdays
prendre (le petit déjeuner, etc)	to have (breakfast, etc)	*normalement	normally
préparer	to prepare	partout	everywhere
quitter (la maison)	to leave (home)	*pas grand-chose	not much
ranger	to tidy/put away	quelquefois	sometimes
		*rarement	rarely
se raser	to have a shave	souvent	often
recevoir	to receive/to get	toujours	always
réveiller (quelqu'un)	to wake (someone) up	tous les (jours) (matins) (soirs) (week-ends)	every (day) (morning) (evening) (weekend)
se réveiller	to wake up		
sortir (la poubelle)	to take out (the dustbin)		
surveiller (un enfant)	to keep an eye on (a child)		
*tondre (le gazon)	to mow (the lawn)		

1 Put these everyday activities in order.

a se coucher   se lever   se réveiller   se laver   se déshabiller

b débarrasser la table   dîner   faire la vaisselle   mettre la table
   faire la cuisine

2 Find the French for five activities you do outside the house.

3 How often do you help at home? Fill in the missing letters.

a s _ _ v _ _ t   d r _ r _ m _ n _

b d _ t _ _ p s e _ _ e m _ _   e t _ _ s l _ s j _ _ _ s

c t _ _ j _ _ r _

4 Find the odd word/phrase out in the following lists.

a se laver   se réveiller   se brosser les dents   se peigner   se raser

b rasoir   aspirateur   table   tondeuse   fer à repasser

c courses   lessive   vaisselle   ménage   argent de poche

d jardinage   dîner   petit déjeuner   déjeuner   goûter

5 Fill in the blanks with the appropriate verb.

demande   me lève   range   prépare   reçois

a En semaine je .... à 7h30, mais le week-end je fais la grasse matinée.

b Le samedi, je .... le petit déjeuner pour ma mère.

c Quelquefois ma mère me .... de faire les courses.

d Si je fais la vaisselle, je .... de l'argent de poche.

e Je .... ma chambre tous les week-ends.

6 Your mum wants help in the house. What does she tell you to do?

Fill in the missing words.

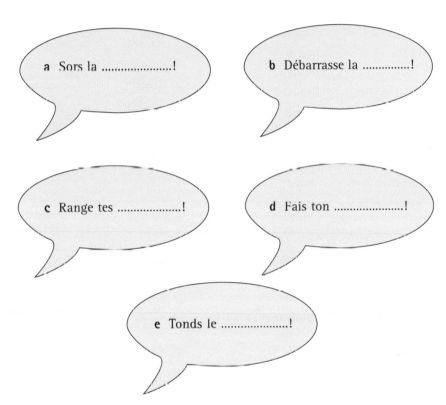

a Sors la ....!

b Débarrasse la ....!

c Range tes ....!

d Fais ton ....!

e Tonds le ....!

7 Replace the pictures in these sentences with the appropriate French word(s).

a Je passe

b Je me

c Je fais

d Je prends

e Je fais

l'anniversaire (de mariage)	birthday (wedding anniversary)	*une alliance	wedding ring
le cadeau	present/gift	la boum	party
*le champagne	champagne	la bûche de Noël	Yule log
*le chant de Noël	Xmas carol	la carte (de Noël)	(Xmas) card
*le curé	priest	*la cérémonie	ceremony
un époux	husband	la chanson	song
le feu d'artifice	firework display	*la coutûme	custom
le fiancé	fiancé	*la dragée	sugared almond
*le garçon d'honneur	best man	*la demoiselle d'honneur	bridesmaid
le gâteau (d'anniversaire)	(birthday) cake	une église	church
*l' hymne national	national anthem	une épouse	wife
le jour de l'an	New Year's Day	la fête	(saint's) name day
le jour de fête	holiday	la fête	festival/ celebration/ party
le jour de Noël	Xmas Day	la fête des Mères	Mother's Day
le jour de congé	day off	la fête du village	village fête
le jour férié	public (bank) holiday	la fête nationale	French national day (Bastille Day)
le maire	mayor	*la fête foraine	funfair
le mariage	marriage	*les fiançailles	engagement (party)
*le marié	bridegroom	la mairie	town hall
un œuf	an egg	*la mariée	bride
le père Noël	Father Xmas	*la Marseillaise	French national anthem
le quatorze juillet	14th July	la messe (de minuit)	(midnight) mass
*le réveillon	Xmas Eve/New Year's Eve meal	les noces (d'argent)	wedding (silver wedding anniversary)
le sapin de Noël	Xmas tree		
*le vin d'honneur	reception (where wine is served)		

la Saint-Nicolas	Saint Nicholas' day
*la Saint-Sylvestre	New Year's Eve
*la Saint-Valentin	Saint Valentine's Day
la surprise-partie	party
les vacances (pl) (de Pâques, etc)	(Easter etc) holidays

célébrer	to celebrate
chanter	to sing
décorer	to decorate
donner	to give
envoyer	to send
faire la bise (à)	to kiss
*faire la fête	to have a party/ to have fun
féliciter	to congratulate
fêter	to celebrate
*se fiancer	to get engaged
*klaxonner	to hoot (car horns)
*se marier (avec)	to get married (to)
offrir	to offer
ouvrir	to open
recevoir	to receive
*trinquer	to clink glasses

Bonne année!	Happy New Year!
Bon anniversaire!	Happy Birthday!

Bon appétit!	Enjoy your meal!
Bonne fête!	Happy name-day!
Bonne journée!	Have a nice day!
Bonne soirée!	Have a nice evening!
Bon voyage!	Have a good journey!
Félicitations!	Congratulations!
Joyeux Noël!	Merry Xmas
Meilleurs vœux!	Best Wishes!
*Santé!	Cheers!
*A la tienne/vôtre (à) Noël (à) Pâques (à) la Pentecôte	Good Health! (at) Xmas (at) Easter (at) Whitsun

agréable	pleasant
autour de (la table)	round (the table)
beaucoup (de)	many/a lot (of)
*civil(e)	civil (i.e. non-religious)
depuis (... ans)	for (... years)
en chocolat	(made of) chocolate
heureux (euse)	happy
*marié(e)	married
*religieux (euse)	religious

1 Put the appropriate festival with these dates.

a le 14 février   b le 14 juillet   c le 25 décembre   d le 31 décembre

2 Which celebration do you associate these words with?

a carte   cadeaux   boum   gâteau   âge

b sapin   chant   messe de minuit   réveillon   bûche

c vin d'honneur   mariée   mairie   demoiselle d'honneur   champagne

3 What do you say to someone...

a on January 1st?

b when they are about to start a meal?

c when it's their birthday?

d when they tell you they're engaged?

e when they're off on holiday?

f on Christmas day?

4 Fill in the missing words in these sentences.

en chocolat   klaxonnent   feu d'artifice   carte   cadeaux

a En route pour le mariage, toutes les voitures ....

b Le Père Noël apporte des .... pour les enfants.

c Le 14 juillet, il y a un grand ....

d A Pâques, on donne des œufs ....

e A la Saint-Valentin, je donne un cadeau et une .... à ma petite amie.

5 Find the French words to fit these definitions.

a The bridegroom's best friend.

b This comes after 25 years of marriage.

c What you say when you drink to someone's health.

d You send your mum a card on this day.

e The bride and groom exchange these.

6 Fill in the crossword, and find another wedding word.

a All French people must go here to get married.

b The drink usually associated with special celebrations.

c The female half of the happy couple.

d After the ceremony comes the ... d'honneur.

e The other half of the couple.

f This sort of ceremony might take place in a church.

g ... and might be held here.

7 Fill in the missing verbs in these sentences.

envoie	fête	ouvrir	fait la bise	recevoir

a Demain, je .... mes 18 ans.

b J'espère que je vais .... beaucoup de cadeaux.

c J'................ des cartes à toutes mes amies.

d J'adore .... les cadeaux le jour de Noël.

e Quand on rencontre des amis, on leur ....

un abricot	apricot	le pain (grillé)	bread (toasted)
l'agneau	lamb	le pamplemousse	grapefruit
un ananas	pineapple	le pâté	pâté
le beurre	butter	les petits pois (pl)	peas
le biscuit	biscuit	*le poireau	leek
le bœuf	beef	le poisson	fish
le bonbon	sweet	le poivre	pepper
le cassis	blackcurrant	*le poivron (rouge)	(red) pepper
le champignon	mushroom	le porc	pork
les chips (pl)	crisps	le pot	pot/jar
le chocolat (chaud)	(hot) chocolate	le potage	soup
le chou	cabbage	le poulet	chicken
le chou de Bruxelles	Brussels sprouts	*le produit	product
le chou-fleur	cauliflower	le raisin	grapes
le citron	lemon	le riz	rice
*le cognac	brandy	le rôti (de bœuf)	roast (beef)
*le concombre	cucumber	le saucisson	(salami-type) sausage
le croissant	croissant	le sel	salt
*les épinards (pl)	spinach	les spaghettis (pl)	spaghetti
les fruits (pl)	fruit	le steak	steak
le gâteau	cake	le sucre	sugar
le gras	fat	le thon	tuna
les haricots verts (pl)	green beans	le toast	toast
le jambon	ham	le veau	veal
*le jus	sauce/gravy	*le végétarisme	vegetarianism
le lait	milk	le vinaigre	vinegar
*le légume	vegetable	le yaourt	yoghurt
le miel	honey		
un œuf	egg		
un oignon	onion		

la baguette	French loaf	la salade (verte)	(green) salad
la banane	banana	la sardine	sardine
la boîte	can/tin	la sauce	sauce
la carotte	carrot	la saucisse	sausage
les céréales (pl)	cereal	la soupe	soup
la cerise	cherry	la tartine	slice of bread
la confiture	jam	la tomate	tomato
la côtelette	chop	la viande	meat
la dinde	turkey		
l'eau (minérale)	(mineral) water	aimer	to like
la farine	flour	avoir faim	to be hungry
la fraise	strawberry	avoir soif	to be thirsty
la framboise	raspberry	boire	to drink
les frites (pl)	chips	détester	to hate
la glace	ice-cream	*éplucher	to peel
l'huile	oil	être	to be
la laitue	lettuce	manger	to eat
la limonade	lemonade		
la moutarde	mustard	*allergique (à)	allergic (to)
la noix	walnut	*dégoûtant(e)	disgusting
la nourriture	food	délicieux(euse)	delicious
une omelette	omelette	*laitier(ière)	dairy
une orange	orange	piquant(e)	spicy
les pâtes (pl)	pasta	*salé(e)	salted/savoury
la pâtisserie	pastry/cake	*végétarien(ne)	vegetarian
la pêche	peach		
*la poêle	frying pan		
la poire	pear		
la pomme	apple		
la pomme de terre	potato		
la purée	puree/mash		

1 Put these items of food in the appropriate column.

poulet   fraise   pomme de terre   poire   agneau   bœuf   petits pois
citron   épinards   saucisson   pamplemousse   poireau

Fruit	Légume	Viande

2 Find the odd word out in each of these lists:

a huile   moutarde   limonade   vinaigre   poivre

b sardine   croissant   pain   beurre   toast

c concombre   haricots verts   petits pois   chou   agneau

d pâtes   chocolat   riz   pommes de terre   pain

3 List these ingredients in the correct column.

œufs poivre sucre fruits oignon pâtes
pommes de terre   sel   farine   confiture

Potage	Gâteau

4 **Complete these excuses for not eating what you are offered.**

   a Non merci, je n'ai pas ....

   b Non merci, je suis ....

   c Non merci, je n'............. pas les épinards.

   d Non merci, je suis .... au poisson.

5 **Which of these items would a really strict vegetarian or a vegan be unable to eat or drink?**

un œuf   le thon   les spaghettis   les céréales   le lait   le yaourt

6 **Match the halves.**

   a nourr...   **i** ...isson

   b sauc...   **ii** ...boise

   c côte...   **iii** ...ignon

   d champ...   **iv** ...lette

   e fram...   **v** ...iture

7 **Find six things to eat in this wordsearch.**

T	S	K	B	R	V	L	D	X
C	O	N	C	O	M	B	R	E
Q	R	M	P	D	Z	J	O	P
S	L	L	A	I	T	U	E	U
N	D	Y	R	T	R	F	U	A
B	H	U	I	L	E	N	F	C
O	I	G	N	O	N	S	S	E

l'ail	garlic	le légume	vegetable
*un apéritif	aperitif (drink)	le menu (à ... francs/ euros)	(... franc/euro) menu
le bifteck	steak	à prix fixe	fixed price menu
le bol	bowl		
le café (-crème)	(white) coffee	enfant	children's menu
le canard	duck		
*le casse-croûte	snack	le melon	melon
le cidre	cider	un orangina	orange drink (brand name)
le coca (cola)	coca-cola		
*le coq (au vin)	coq au vin (chicken in wine sauce)	le parfum	flavour
		le plat	dish (food)
*les coquillages (pl)	shellfish	*le plat cuisiné	take-away dish
le couteau	knife	le plat du jour	today's special
le couvert	place setting	le plat principal	main course
le crabe	crab	le pourboire	tip
le croque-monsieur	ham & cheese toasted sandwich	le restaurant	restaurant
		le sandwich	sandwich
		le saumon	salmon
le croque-madame	with fried egg on top	le service	service
		le steak-frites	steak and chips
le dessert	dessert/ pudding		
		le thé (au lait)	tea (with milk)
un escargot	snail	le verre	glass
le fast-food	fast food (restaurant)	le vin	wine
le fromage	cheese	l'addition	bill
le fruit	fruit	une assiette	plate
les fruits de mer (pl)	seafood	*une assiette anglaise	assorted cold meats
le garçon (de café)	waiter		
un hamburger	hamburger	une assiette de crudités	assorted raw vegetables
un hors-d'œuvre	starter		
le jus (de fruit)	(fruit) juice	la bière	beer

la boisson	drink	la vanille	vanilla
la bouteille	bottle		
la cafetière	coffee pot	commander	to order
*la cafétéria	cafeteria	commencer	to start/begin
la carafe	jug/carafe	prendre	to have (food/ drink)
la carte	menu		
la cerise	cherry	à la carte	choice from menu
la charcuterie	cooked meats		
la côte de porc	pork chop	... à la fraise (etc)	strawberry ...
la crème	cream	*à point	medium rare
la crêpe	pancake	bien cuit(e)	well done
la crêperie	pancake restaurant	chinois(e)	Chinese
		(non) compris(e)	(not) included
la crevette	prawn	garni(e)	including vegetables
les crudités	assorted raw vegetables		
la cuiller	spoon	(tarte) maison	home-made (tart)
une douzaine de	a dozen	(yaourt) nature	natural/plain (yoghurt)
*une entrecôte	steak		
la fourchette	fork	pour commencer	to start with
la glace	ice-cream	propre	clean
*la grillade	grilled meat	*saignant(e)	rare
*les huîtres (pl)	oysters	sale	dirty
les moules (pl)	mussels		
la pizza	pizza	Mademoiselle!	Miss! (to waitress)
la pizzeria	pizzeria	Monsieur!	(to call waiter)
la spécialité	speciality	Qu'est-ce que c'est le/la ...?	What is ...?
la tarte (aux pommes)	(apple) tart		
la tasse	cup	C'est quoi le/la ...?	What is ...?
la terrasse	terrace		
la truite	trout		

1 Which is the odd word out in the following lists?

a cafétéria   restaurant   café-crème   crêperie   pizzeria

b coquillages   fruits de mer   moules   huîtres   entrecôte

c cuiller   fourchette   couvert   couteau   dessert

d légume   carafe   tasse   verre   bol

e bière   melon   cidre   orangina   jus de fruit

2 Match the halves.

a une douzaine d'...   i ... vin rouge

b une carafe de ...   ii ... aux cerises

c une bouteille d' ...   iii ... escargots

d une tarte ...   iv ... crudités

e une assiette de ...   v ... orangina

3 Put these items in the right place on the menu.

tarte maison

service

côte de porc

compris

hors-d'œuvre

Potage
ou
a ....

Steak-frites
ou
b ....

Glace
ou
c ....
1/4 de vin rouge d ....
e .... 15% non-compris

4 Find the French word which fits each of these definitions.

a Money you give the waiter for good service.

b A drink before the meal.

c Toasted cheese and ham sandwich.

d Describes a plain yoghurt.

e A very, very under-cooked piece of meat!

5 Fill in the gaps in this conversation at a restaurant.

plat principal   boisson   bouteille   pour commencer   carte
monsieur   commander

CLIENT   Monsieur, la **a** .... s'il vous plaît.

GARÇON   Vous voulez **b** .... maintenant ?

CLIENT   **c** ...., je prends le potage.

GARÇON   Oui, **d** ....,,

CLIENT   Et comme **e** ...., je voudrais le coq au vin.

GARÇON   Et comme **f** .... ?

CLIENT   Une **g** .... de vin rouge.

6 Solve the anagrams to find five snacks/fast-foods.

   a zipaz   **b** brumharge   **c** wasncihd   **d** pêrce   **e** sacse-trocûe

7 Find seven things you would see, but could not eat, in the restaurant.

A	D	D	I	T	I	O	N	R
C	M	K	E	F	B	C	H	V
P	O	U	R	B	O	I	R	E
C	C	U	I	L	L	E	R	R
W	Q	O	V	D	P	U	I	R
I	A	S	S	E	S	T	L	E
W	C	J	K	O	R	F	B	R
P	A	S	S	I	E	T	T	E

un adolescent	adolescent	se droguer	to take drugs
l'alcool	alcohol	éviter	to avoid
*un athlète	athlete	fumer	to smoke
*le cancer	cancer	s'habituer (à)	to get used to
le cœur	heart	*menacer	to threaten
le danger	danger	mourir	to die
le drogué	drug addict	persuader	to persuade
*le gosse	kid (child)	refuser	to refuse
les jeunes (pl)	young people	regretter	to regret
*les poumons (pl)	lungs	*renoncer (à)	to give up
le régime	diet	risquer (de)	to risk
le risque	risk	rouler	to travel/drive
le sport	sport	savoir	to know
le tabac	tobacco	suivre	to follow
*le taux (d'alcool)	alcohol level		

la cigarette	cigarette	au volant	at the (steering) wheel
*la crise cardiaque	heart attack	dangereux	dangerous
la drogue	drugs	en (bonne) forme	fit
l'exercice	exercise	*équilibré(e)	balanced
la forme	fitness	gros(se)	fat
une habitude	habit	important(e)	important
*les matières grasses (pl)	fats	*imprudent(e)	unwise
*la prévention routière	road safety	*inadmissible	unacceptable
la réaction	reaction	*ivre	drunk
la santé	health	lent(e)	slow
		malheureux(euse)	unhappy
		malheureusement	unfortunately
conduire	to drive	*pire	worse
courir	to run	trop	too (much)

1 Fill in the blanks in these sentences.

> dangereux   éviter   alcool   régime   refuser
> crise cardiaque   en forme   fumez

a Si vous ...., vous devez renoncer pour .... le cancer.

b Vous ne devez pas boire d'............. avant de conduire.

c Si vous mangez trop de matières grasses, vous risquez une ....

d L'alcool est .... au volant.

e Vous devez toujours .... la drogue.

f Pour rester ...., il est important d'avoir un .... équilibré.

2 Fill in the missing letters to find four positive words about healthy living.

a s _ _ _ é   b s _ _ _ t   c e _ _ _ _ _ _ e   d é _ _ _ _ _ _ _ é

3 Find the French word which fits each of these definitions.

a Personne qui fait beaucoup de sport.

b Personne qui a entre 10 et 16 ans.

c Personne qui a l'habitude de se droguer.

4 Find the opposites of these words.

a heureux   b acceptable   c prudent   d rapide   e sans risques

French	English	French	English
un acteur	actor	*le fric	cash (slang)
un annuaire	telephone directory	*le gérant	manager
		un informaticien	computer scientist
le boucher	butcher		
le boulanger	baker	le (petit) job	(part-time) job
le boulot	job (slang)	*le PDG (président-directeur-général)	managing director
le bureau	office		
le chanteur	singer	le journal	newspaper
*le classeur	filing cabinet	*le licenciement	redundancy, dismissal
*le clavier	keyboard		
le client	customer	*le logiciel	software
le coiffeur	hairdresser	le maçon	builder
le collègue	colleague	le mannequin	model
le commerçant	shopkeeper	le mécanicien	mechanic
*le contrat	contract	le message	message
le coup de téléphone	phone call	le métier	trade/job/craft
le courrier (électronique)	mail (electronic)	un ouvrier	worker
		le patron	boss
*le curseur	cursor	le propriétaire	owner
le directeur	manager	le répondeur	answering machine
un écran	screen		
un électricien	electrician	le salaire	salary
un e-mail	e-mail	le serveur	waiter
un emploi	job	le stage	work experience
un employé	employee/clerk		
un employeur	employer	*le traitement de texte	word-processing
un entretien	interview	le travail	work
un épicier	grocer	le vendeur	salesman
*un établissement	establishment/firm		
		une actrice	actress
le fermier	farmer	une annonce	advert
*le fichier	filing cabinet	*une augmentation	increase

la carrière	career	taper (une lettre)	to type (a letter)
la chanteuse	singer	(taper à la	(to do (some)
la conférence	meeting/	machine)	typing)
	conference	travailler	to work
la disquette	floppy disk	utiliser	to use
une équipe	team		
*la fiche	form	Allô	Hello (on
la formation	training		phone)
*une imprimante	printer	*(un contrat)	fixed term
la machine à écrire	typewriter	à durée déterminée	(contract)
la photocopie	photocopy	à l'appareil	speaking (on
la profession	profession		the phone)
la réunion	meeting	de bonne heure	early
une usine	factory	de la part de (qui?)	from (whom?)
		dur(e)	hard
		essentiel(le)	essential
*augmenter	to increase	fatigant(e)	tiring
choisir	to choose	fatigué(e)	tired
*classer	to file	*financier(ière)	financial
connaître	to know	ne quittez pas	hold the line
*se débrouiller	to manage/to	sans	without
	cope	varié(e)	varied
déranger	to disturb		
devenir	to become		
distribuer	to deliver		
faire dans la vie	to do for a		
	living		
faire des économies	to save up		
*imprimer	to print		
*licencier	to sack/dismiss		
livrer	to deliver		
organiser	to organise		
rappeler	to call back		

1 Find the odd word out in each of the following lists.

a message   coup de téléphone   emploi   e-mail   courrier

b imprimante   salaire   clavier   écran   curseur

c employé   patron   gérant   PDG   employeur

d répondeur   conférence   classeur   machine à écrire   fichier

e client   collègue   commerçant   journal   fermier

2 Complete this grid.

acteur	actrice
a	chanteuse
b	employée
c	ouvrière
d	bouchère
e	coiffeuse
f	directrice
g	informaticienne

3 Fill in the missing vowels to find five things you might use at work.

a d _ s q _ _ t t _   b p h _ t _ c _ p _ _   c f _ c h _   d c l _ v _ _ r
e l _ g _ c _ _ l

4 Find a French word to fit each of these definitions.

a Being made unemployed.

b The sort of learning you do at work.

c Place where people work to make things.

d Chat with a prospective employer.

e What you sign when you get a job.

f Group of people who work together.

5 Complete the crossword, and find another job.

   a He sells meat.

   b She works for someone else.

   c He works on the land.

   d She appears in plays and films.

   e He styles hair.

   f He/She shows off clothes.

   g He fixes lights etc.

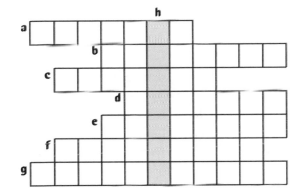

6 Fill in the gaps in this telephone conversation.

> quittez   rappeler   part   allô   directeur

SECRETAIRE	**a** ....
MADAME LEGRAND	Je voudrais parler au **b** ....
SECRETAIRE	C'est de la **c** .... de qui ?
MADAME LEGRAND	Madame Legrand.
SECRETAIRE	Ne **d** .... pas, madame. ... Je regrette, le directeur est absent. Il peut vous **e** .... ?

7 Solve the anagrams to find four words connected with money.

   a relaisa   **b** mantreuge   **c** omonécies   **d** crif

*l'alpinisme	mountaineering
*l'athlétisme	athletics
le bal	dance
le basket	basketball
le CD	CD
le centre sportif	sports/leisure centre
*le clavier	keyboard
le complexe sportif	sports/leisure centre
le concert	concert
le concours	competition
*le court de tennis	tennis court
le cyclisme	cycling
le disque (compact)	record (compact disc)
*les échecs (pl)	chess
le foot(ball)	football
le groupe	group
le handball	handball
le hockey	hockey
le jeu (vidéo)	(video) game
le loisir	leisure
le match	match
le membre	member
*le musicien	musician
un orchestre	orchestra
le passe-temps	hobby/pastime
le patinage	skating
le patin (à roulettes/ sur glace)	(roller/ice) skating
le piano	piano

le rendez-vous	date
le roman	novel
le rugby	rugby
le ski (nautique)	(water) skiing
le stade	stadium/ground
le tennis (de table)	tennis (table-tennis)
le terrain	pitch
le violon	violin
le volley	volleyball
le VTT	mountain bike
le zoo	zoo

la bande dessinée	cartoon
*la batterie	drums
*la boîte (de nuit)	(night) club
les boules (pl)	(French) bowls
la canne à pêche	fishing rod
les cartes (pl)	cards
la cassette (vidéo)	(video) cassette
*la course (automobile)	race/racing (motor race/ racing)
la danse	dancing
la discothèque	disco
*l'escrime	fencing
une équipe	team
l'équitation	horse-riding
la flûte (à bec)	flute (recorder)
la guitare	guitar
la gymnastique	gymnastics

la lecture	reading	jouer à	to play (+ sport/game)
*la Maison des Jeunes (la MJC)	Youth Club	(jouer au tennis)	(to play tennis)
la musique (pop/classique/rock)	(pop/classical/ rock) music	jouer de	to play (+ instrument)
la natation	swimming	(jouer de la batterie)	(to play the drums)
la partie (de)	game (of)	lire	to read
*la passion	passion/main interest	nager	to swim
la patinoire	skating rink	*participer	to take part in
la pêche	fishing	passionner	to fascinate
la photographie	photography	*pratiquer (un sport)	to take part in/play (sport)
la piscine	swimming baths	se promener	to go for a walk
la planche (à voile) (à roulettes)	wind-surfing (skate-boarding)	regarder	to watch
la promenade (à vélo/en bateau)	walk(ing) (bike/boat ride)	surfer sur internet	to surf the net
la randonnée	rambling	*doué(e) (pour)	gifted/good (at)
la surprise	surprise	fana(tique)	fan(atical)
la trompette	trumpet	favori(te)	favourite
la voile	sailing	passionnant(e)	exciting
		sportif(ive)	sporty

aller à la pêche	to go fishing
avoir lieu	to take place
danser	to dance
écouter	to listen (to)
faire (+ activities not played)	to go, do
(faire du patin)	(to go skating)
faire partie de	to belong to

1 Find the French game/sport which fits these definitions.

   a You fight your opponent with swords.

   b Played on a board with 64 squares.

   c A cross between basketball and 5-a-side football.

   d You play with 52 of these.

   e Often played on the beach – even in the Olympics!

2 Find six musical instruments in this wordsearch.

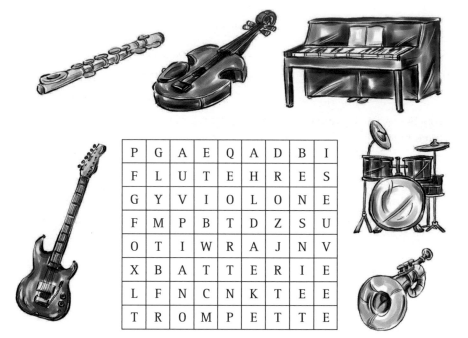

P	G	A	E	Q	A	D	B	I
F	L	U	T	E	H	R	E	S
G	Y	V	I	O	L	O	N	E
F	M	P	B	T	D	Z	S	U
O	T	I	W	R	A	J	N	V
X	B	A	T	T	E	R	I	E
L	F	N	C	N	K	T	E	E
T	R	O	M	P	E	T	T	E

3 Fill in the missing letters to find five leisure activities.

   a l _ _ _ _ r e   **c** v _ _ _ e   **e** p _ _ _ _ n _ _ e

   b p _ _ _ o _ _ _ p _ _ _   **d** c _ _ _ _ _ m e

4 Complete the following sentences with an appropriate adjective.

a Je suis .... de rugby.

b David Ginola est très .... pour le football.

c Mon sport ...., c'est le tennis.

d L'équitation est ....

e Je ne suis pas très ....

5 Which is the odd word out in each of the following lists?

a patin à roulettes   ski nautique   planche à voile   natation   voile

b danse   discothèque   orchestre   piscine   musique

c cyclisme   concert   VTT   course automobile   équitation

d stade   passe-temps   MJC   complexe sportif   terrain

6 Complete the following sentences with the appropriate verb.

écouter   danser   avoir lieu   lire   nager

a Le concert va .... le 8 septembre.

b J'adore .... à la piscine.

c Je préfère .... mes CD.

d J'aime ....des romans.

e Ce soir, je vais .... dans une boîte de nuit.

7 Solve the following clues.

a Personne qui joue dans un orchestre.

b On pratique ce sport en montagne.

c Un concours entre deux équipes.

d Stade spécial où on fait du patin à glace.

un acteur	actor	l'orchestre	stalls (downstairs seats)
*un animateur	presenter	*le polar	cop film/story
*un article	article	*le présentateur	presenter
le balcon	balcony	*le rédacteur	editor
le cinéma	cinema	*le roman-photo	photo-romance
*le courrier du cœur	agony column	*le sous-titre	sub-title
le dessin animé	cartoon (film)	le spectacle	show
le documentaire	documentary	*le téléfilm	TV film
*le DVD	DVD	le téléspectateur	viewer
un écran	screen	le théâtre	theatre
*le fait divers	(unimportant) news story	*le tube	hit record
*le feuilleton	soap/serial	le (gros) titre	headline
le film	film		
(comique)	(comedy)	*les actualités	current affairs
(d'amour)	(love story)	*une antenne (parabolique)	aerial (satellite dish)
(d'aventures)	(adventure)	*la caméra	(film/tv camera)
(d'épouvante)	(horror)	*la causerie télévisée	chat show
(d'horreur)	(horror)	la chaîne	channel
(de science fiction)	(science fiction)	une émission (de sport)	(sports) programme
(policier)	(crime)	une image	picture
(western)	(cowboy)	les informations (pl) (les infos)	news
*le flash (d'information) (-info)	news flash	la page	page
*le jeu télévisé	game show	*la parole	word
le journal	newspaper	la pièce (de théâtre)	play
*le journal télévisé	television news	la place	seat
le journaliste	journalist	la presse	press
*le lecteur	reader	la publicité (la pub)	advert/ advertising
le magazine	magazine		
*le metteur en scène	director		

la radio	radio	rire	to laugh
la revue	(glossy) magazine	*tourner un film	to make a film
la salle (cinéma à 5 salles)	auditorium (5-screen cinema)	*traiter de	to deal with
la scène	stage	amusant(e)	amusing
la séance	performance/ show	drôle	funny
la série	series	en couleur	in colour
la télévision (par satellite) (*par câble)	television (satellite) (cable)	en noir et blanc	in black and white
la une (à la une)	front page (on the front page)	il s'agit de...	it's about ...
		libre (radio libre)	independent (independent radio)
*la tournée	tour (of singer etc)	local(e)	local
la vedette	(film) star	plusieurs	several
la version (française)	(French) version/ soundtrack	romantique	romantic
(originale)	(original soundtrack)	sous-titré(e)	sub-titled

s'amuser	to have a good time
*applaudir	to applaud
avoir peur	to be frightened
*effrayer	to frighten
faire peur à	to frighten
passer à (la radio/la télé)	to be on (radio/TV)
plaire (le film m'a plu)	to please (I liked the film)

20 Media (cinema, television, theatre)

1 Put these words into the appropriate column.

scène   téléspectateur   informations   pièce   balcon
sous-titre   feuilleton   applaudir

Télévision	Théâtre

2 Find the odd word out in each of these lists.

a satellite   place   Canal+   téléfilm   câble

b article   page   roman-photo   radio   fait divers

c policier   courrier du cœur   comique   aventures   horreur

d image   lecteur   rédacteur   journaliste   présentateur

e journal   caméra   magazine   revue   presse

3 Complete the following sentences.

amour   sous-titrés   épouvante   en noir et blanc   comiques

a J'aime bien les films d'..................... . Ils me font peur.

b J'aime les films .... Je les trouve drôles.

c Je n'aime pas les films d'............. . Ils sont trop romantiques.

d Je n'aime pas les films étrangers. Ils sont ....

e Je n'aime pas les vieux films. Ils sont ....

4 Solve the anagrams to find five words to do with broadcasting.

   a simiéons   **b** ementocairdu   **c** clubpitéi   **d** éries   **e** înecha

5 Find a French word/phrase to fit each of these definitions.

   a Letters to a magazine talking about problems.

   b Members of the public appear in this to win prizes.

   c The most important actor in a film.

   d Series of drawings which give a moving picture.

   e Newspapers, magazines, radio, tv etc.

6 Find seven different types of film in this wordsearch.

C	D	F	P	R	L	W	N	E	S
P	H	A	G	F	E	E	T	P	C
A	O	C	M	L	E	S	R	O	O
B	R	L	N	O	S	T	P	U	M
X	R	V	I	T	U	E	L	V	I
Q	E	N	E	C	T	R	M	A	Q
M	U	F	Y	S	I	N	Q	N	U
N	R	P	T	L	V	E	R	T	E
C	A	V	E	N	T	U	R	E	S

7 Fill in the missing letters to find five words to do with the cinema.

   a s _ _ _ e   **c** é _ _ _ n   **e** b _ _ _ _ n

   b p _ _ _ r   **d** s _ _ _ - _ _ _ _ e

l'amour	love
*un auteur	author
le bijou	jewel
le but	goal
le caractère	personality
le champion	champion
le championnat	championship
le chanteur	singer
*le comportement	behaviour
le courage	courage
*un écrivain	writer
*le footballeur	footballer
*le héros	hero
un homme	man
le joueur (de rugby)	(rugby) player
le peintre	painter
le petit ami	boy-friend
le piercing	(body) piercing
les rapports (pl)	relationship(s)
*le sens de l'humour	sense of humour
*le tableau	painting/ picture
les vêtements (pl)	clothes
le visage	face

la bêtise	something stupid
la chance	luck
la date (de naissance)	(birth) date
la dispute	argument

l'enfance	childhood
la femme	woman
*la haine	hatred
la peinture	painting
la permission	permission
la petite amie	girlfriend

admirer	to admire
se comporter	to behave
critiquer	to criticise
se disputer	to argue
espérer	to hope
s'entendre (avec)	to get on (with)
se fâcher	to get angry
*faire l'idiot	to act the fool
gagner	to win
*imiter	to imitate
*marquer (un but)	to score (a goal)
*ressembler à	to look like
réussir	to succeed

*absolument	absolutely
*accueillant(e)	welcoming
aimable	likeable
amoureux(euse) (de)	in love (with)
*au début	at the beginning
bête	silly
bien	well
*bizarre	odd/strange
*branché(e)	trendy
célèbre	famous

*célibataire	unmarried	*malgré	in spite of
*cependant	however	*merveilleux(euse)	marvellous
charmant(e)	charming	mince	slim
chouette	terrific	méchant(e)	nasty
comme	like	né(e)	born
courageux(euse)	brave	*optimiste	optimistic
cruel(le)	cruel	*ouvert(e)	out-going
*de bonne humeur	in a good mood	paresseux(euse)	lazy
*de mauvaise humeur	in a bad mood	pénible	tiresome
		*pessimiste	pessimistic
*déçu(e)	disappointed	poli(e)	polite
*dernier(ière)	latest	sage	well-behaved
dynamique	energetic	stupide	stupid
égoïste	selfish	sympa(thique)	nice
élégant(e)	elegant	timide	shy/timid
*embêtant(e)	annoying	tout le monde	everybody
excellent(e)	excellent	triste	sad
*extra(ordinaire)	super		
fâché(e)	angry		
*franchement	frankly		
généreux(euse)	generous		
*génial(e)	brilliant		
habillé(e)	dressed		
honnête	honest		
idiot(e)	daft		
impoli(e)	impolite		
*impressionnant(e)	impressive		
intelligent(e)	intelligent		
*jaloux(ouse)	jealous		
joli(e)	pretty		
laid(e)	ugly		
maigre	thin		

1 Put each of these adjectives into the appropriate column.

aimable   cruel   méchant   stupide   généreux

génial   égoïste   charmant   paresseux   courageux

Positif	Négatif

2 Complete the crossword, and find another word for a person.

a Always doing brave deeds.

b Takes part in a game.

c The best of the lot.

d Female person.

e Artist who paints pictures.

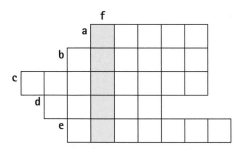

ACTIVITIES

3 Fill in the blanks in these sentences with the appropriate verb.

| ressemble | fâchent | disputé | critiquent | marqué | gagné |

a Je me suis .... avec ma petite amie.

b Mon footballeur préféré a .... le championnat trois fois.

c Il a .... beaucoup de buts.

d Je .... un peu à mon héros.

e Mes parents .... toujours mes vêtements.

f Ils se .... au sujet de mes piercings.

4 Find the opposite of each of these words.

a courageux   b stupide   c impoli   d amour   e joli

5 Find a French word to match each of these descriptions.

a The way a person acts.

b The things people find funny.

c Period of time when one is young.

d The day someone is born.

e The way people interact with each other.

6 Solve the anagrams to find five things you might like about someone.

a cluclantiea   b éranbhc   c quimandyc   d trouve   e honlêne

7 Now fill in the missing letters to find five qualities you might not like about them.

a j _ _ _ _ x   c c _ _ _ l   e b _ _ _ _ _ e

b p _ _ _ _ _ e   d é _ _ _ _ _ e

un échange	exchange
un instant	moment
*le lendemain	next day

l'hospitalité	hospitality
une invitation	invitation
la rencontre	meeting
la visite	visit

accepter	to accept
*accueillir	to welcome
*aller chercher	to fetch
*amener	to bring (someone)
*apporter	to bring (something)
s'asseoir	to sit down
décider	to decide
embrasser	to kiss
emmener	to take (someone) (away)
*être en train de ...	to be busy doing ...
*être sur le point de	to be on the point of
*faire la connaissance	to make the acquaintance
fixer (un rendez-vous)	to arrange (a date)
manquer (le bus)	to miss (the bus)
proposer	to suggest
remercier	to thank

rencontrer	to meet (for the first time, or by chance)
retrouver	to meet
saluer	to greet
*tutoyer	to call someone 'tu'
*venir chercher	to come and call for

A bientôt!	See you soon!
A demain!	See you tomorrow!
A tout à l'heure!	See you later!
Au revoir!	Goodbye!
Bienvenue!	Welcome!
*Bon courage!	Good luck !
Bonjour!	Hello/Good morning!
Bon séjour!	Have a nice stay!
Bonsoir!	Good evening!
Bonne chance!	Good luck!
Bonne nuit!	Good night!
*Désolé(e)!	Sorry!

lundi	Mon	vendredi	Fri
mardi	Tue	samedi	Sat
mercredi	Wed	dimanche	Sun
jeudi	Thurs		

*Enchanté(e)!	Pleased to meet you!
*Entendu!	Agreed!
Salut!	Hi!

*après-demain	the day after tomorrow	Ça va (?)	I'm (Are you?) OK
aujourd'hui	today	certainement	certainly
*avant-hier	the day before yesterday	d'abord	first
		d'accord	OK/All right
ce matin	this morning	dans	in
cet après-midi	this afternoon	dans (dix) minutes	in (ten) minutes
ce soir	tonight	de rien	don't mention it
demain	tomorrow	*en avance	early
hier	yesterday	là	there
		là-bas	over there

janvier	Jan	juillet	July
février	Feb	août	Aug
mars	Mar	septembre	Sept
avril	Apr	octobre	Oct
mai	May	novembre	Nov
juin	Jun	décembre	Dec

au mois de (mai)	in (the month of May)	madame	Madam/Mrs/Ms
		mademoiselle	Miss
en (janvier)	in (January)	maintenant	now
à l'heure	on time	*malheureusement	unfortunately
à part	apart from	merci (pour)	thank you (for)
au bout de (la rue)	at the end of (the street)	monsieur	Sir/Mr
		occupé(e)	busy
au coin (de)	at the corner (of)	pardon	sorry
		*ravi(e)	delighted
au milieu (de)	in the middle (of)	Asseyez-vous! (Assieds-toi!)	Sit down!
		Entre(z)!	Come in!
avec plaisir	with pleasure	Je passerai te chercher	I'll call for you
bien entendu	of course	On se retrouve où?	Where shall we meet ?
bien sûr	of course	(... à quelle heure?)	(What time ...)
bientôt	soon	Si on allait ...	How about going ...
		Voici (Marie)	Here is/This is (Marie)

1 Find the odd word out in each of the following lists.

  a dimanche   août   mardi   mercredi   samedi

  b automne   printemps   aujourd'hui   hiver   été

  c soir   juillet   mars   juin   février

  d invitation   instant   échange   visite   hospitalité

  e Bonjour   Bonsoir   Au revoir   Enchanté   Salut

  f A demain   Bienvenue   Bonne nuit   A tout à l'heure   A bientôt

2 Find a French word or phrase to fit each of these definitions.

  a To arrange an appointment to see someone.

  b To say hello to someone.

  c To be on the point of ...

  d To go to someone's house to pick them up.

  e To fail to catch (e.g. a train).

3 Complete the following sentences with the appropriate verb.

embrassée   proposé   décidé   remercié   accepter

  a Je veux bien .... votre invitation.

  b Il a .... de venir me chercher.

  c Il m'a .... et il a dit « Bon voyage ! »

  d Mon correspondant m'a .... un échange.

  e Je l'ai .... de son hospitalité.

4 Complete these phrases. (They're all about time.)

  a à l'_ _ _ _ _   **d** c _ m _ _ _ _

  b d _ _ _ cinq m _ _ _ _ _ s   **e** le l _ _ _ _ _ _ _ n

  c à q _ _ _ _ _ h _ _ _ _ ?

5 If this is maintenant

lundi
3
septembre
09h30

find the appropriate French word/phrase for each of the following:

samedi
1
septembre

a

dimanche
2
septembre
09h00

b

lundi
3
septembre
15h00

c

mardi
4
septembre
20h00

d

mercredi
5
septembre

e

| après-demain | hier matin | avant-hier | cet après-midi | demain soir |

6 Solve the clues to find the French for six words you might use when accepting an invitation.

a certainly   **b** see you soon   **c** with pleasure   **d** OK   **e** delighted

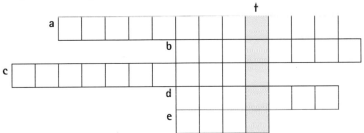

7 Fill in the gaps in the following telephone conversation.

| demain | passerai te chercher | merci | bien sûr | salut | à demain |

THOMAS	Allô, ici Thomas.
SOPHIE	**a**.............., Thomas.
THOMAS	Tu vas à la boum chez Marc **b**................ soir ?
SOPHIE	Oui **c**......................... .
THOMAS	Alors, je **d**..................... à huit heures. **e**................. .
SOPHIE	D'accord. **f**.............. Thomas.

*l'accès	access/entry
les achats (pl)	shopping/ purchases
un appareil photo	camera
un ascenseur	lift
*le bricolage	Do-It-Yourself
*le caméscope	camcorder
le centre commercial	shopping centre
*le chariot	(supermarket) trolley
le choix	choice
le comptoir	counter
le grand magasin	department store
un hypermarché	hypermarket
le jeu (*de société)	(board) game
le jouet	toy
le kiosque à journaux	news stand
le marchand	shopkeeper/ stallholder
le marché	market
le mètre	metre
un opticien	optician
le poids	weight
le porte-clés	key-ring
le prix	price
le rayon (boucherie)	(butchery) department
le reçu	receipt
le self	self-service restaurant

les soldes (pl)	sales
le sous-sol	basement
le souvenir	souvenir
le supermarché	supermarket
le (bureau de) tabac	tobacconist's

une affiche	poster
la boucherie	butcher's
la boulangerie	baker's
la casserole	saucepan
la charcuterie	cooked meat shop
la confiserie	sweet shop
*les conserves (pl)	tinned foods
la crémerie	dairy produce
*la dégustation	tasting
une dizaine	(about) ten
une enveloppe	envelope
une épicerie	grocer's
*une exposition	display/ exhibition
*la fermeture (annuelle)	(annual) closing
la fin	end
*la grande surface	supermarket/ hypermarket
*les heures d'affluence (pl)	rush hour
la librairie	book shop
*la maison de la presse	newsagent's
la monnaie	change
*l'ouverture	opening

la parfumerie	perfume shop	C'est combien?	How much is it?
la pâtisserie	cake shop	Défense de (fumer)	No (smoking)
la pharmacie	chemist's	*disponible	available
la pipe	pipe	*d'occasion	second hand
*la platine laser	CD player	en bois	(made of) wood
la poissonnerie	fish shop	en métal	(made of) metal
la promotion	special offer	en plastique	(made of) plastic
la réduction	reduction		
la vitrine	shop-window	exceptionnel(le)	exceptional
		frais (fraîche)	fresh
acheter	to buy	... grammes de	... grams of
coûter	to cost	gratuit(e)	free
demander	to ask for	interdit(e)	forbidden
dépenser	to spend	Je peux vous aider?	Can I help you?
échanger	to exchange	Je le/la/les prends.	I'll take it/them.
*faire du lèche-vitrine	to go window-shopping	Je voudrais ...	I'd like ...
		Je vous en prie.	It's my pleasure.
*faire un paquet-cadeau	to wrap up as a gift	léger(ère)	light
payer	to pay (for)	(dix) pour cent	(ten) per cent
pousser	to push	(3) pour le prix de (2)	(3) for the price of (2)
*rembourser	to reimburse	réduit(e)	reduced
tirer	to pull	*satisfait(e)	satisfied
vendre	to sell	surgelé(e)	frozen
		un kilo de	a kilo of
affreux(euse)	horrible	un litre de	a litre of
bon marché	cheap	un paquet de	a packet of
cher (chère)	dear/expensive		
combien	how many/ how much		

1 Which is the odd one out in each of the following lists?

a comptoir   porte-clés   pipe   jouet   souvenir

b grande surface   centre commercial   supermarché   chariot
grand magasin

c bureau de tabac   boucherie   librairie   maison de la presse
kiosque à journaux

d monnaie   prix exceptionnel   réduction   soldes   promotion

e défense d'entrer   léger   interdit   poussez   tirez

2 Match the halves.

a un kilo de ...   **i**   ... jambon

b un litre de ...   **ii**   ... plastique

c un paquet de ...   **iii**   ... carottes

d 200 grammes de ...   **iv**   ... chips

e un jouet en ...   **v**   ... vin rouge

3 Complete the crossword with six names of shops – and find another place to buy things.

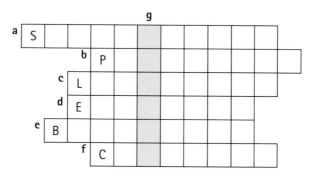

4 Fill in the missing vowels to find five non-food items.

   a p l _ t _ n _ l _ s _ r   **c** j _ _ _ _ s _ c _ _ t _   **e** _ n v _ l _ p p _

   b c _ m _ s c _ p _   **d** _ p p _ r _ _ l p h _ t _

5 Find a French word to fit each of these definitions.

   a The busiest time of the day on the roads.

   b To make into an attractive parcel.

   c Period when the shopkeeper is away for his yearly holiday.

   d Person who checks your eyesight.

   e Chance to try products such as wine, cheese, etc.

6 Complete the following announcements which you might hear in a supermarket.

promotion	achetez	réduction	gratuit	pour le prix de deux

a .... de quinze pour cent au rayon librairie.

b Trois CD ....

c .... sur tous les jouets.

d .... trois porte-clés, recevez un quatrième **e** ....

7 Solve the anagrams to find five ways of describing goods.

   a faruxef   **b** duirét   **c** chefaîr   **d** scad'oconi   **e** onb craméh

un anorak	anorak
les bas (pl)	stockings
le blouson	(short) jacket
le bonnet	woolly hat
le bouton	button
le chapeau	hat
*le chausson	slipper
le chemisier	blouse
le collant	tights
*le corsage	blouse
le costume	suit
le coton	cotton
le foulard	scarf
les gants (pl)	gloves
le gant de toilette	flannel
le gilet	waistcoat, cardigan
un imperméable (un imper)	mac/raincoat
le jean	jeans
le jogging	tracksuit
*le lavage à la main	hand-washing
*le look	image/fashion
le maillot (de bain)	swimming costume
le manteau	coat
*le mouchoir	handkerchief
*le nettoyage à sec	dry-cleaning
le nylon	nylon
le pantalon	trousers
le pardessus	overcoat
le parfum	perfume

le pull(over)	sweater/ pullover
le rouge à lèvres	lipstick
le short	shorts
le slip (de bain)	underpants (swimming trunks)
le soutien-gorge	bra
le survêtement	tracksuit
le sweat-shirt	sweat-shirt
le T-shirt	T-shirt
le tricot	jumper
les vêtements (pl)	clothes

les baskets (pl)	trainers
les bottes (pl)	boots
la casquette	cap
la ceinture	belt
les chaussettes (pl)	socks
les chaussures (pl)	shoes
la chemise	shirt
*la chemise de nuit	nightie
la cravate	tie
la culotte	panties
une écharpe	scarf
*la fermeture éclair	zip-fastener
*la gamme	range
la jupe	skirt
la laine	wool
la mode	fashion
la paire	pair
*la pointure	size (of shoes)

la robe	dress	court(e)	short
la robe de chambre	dressing gown	*déchiré(e)	torn
les sandales (pl)	sandals	*de marque	branded
la taille	size (of clothes)	*dépassé(e)	out of date
la veste	jacket	en coton	in cotton
		en (trente-neuf)	in (size 39)
essayer	to try (on)	en (noir)	in (black)
*manquer (il manque un bouton)	to lack (there's a button missing)	en (laine)	in (wool)
		*étroit(e)	narrow
		*griffé(e)	designer
mettre	to put on	long(ue)	long
porter	to wear	lourd(e)	heavy
*rétrécir	to shrink	Quelle pointure?	What size? (for shoes)
blanc (blanche)	white	Quelle taille?	What size? (for clothes)
bleu(e)	blue	rayé(e)	striped
brun(e)	brown	serré(e)	tight
gris(e)	grey	*uni(e)	plain/self-coloured
jaune	yellow		
noir(e)	black		
rose	pink		
rouge	red		
vert(e)	green		
violet(te)	violet		
(bleu) clair	light (blue)		
(vert) foncé	dark (green)		
(rouge) vif	bright (red)		
*à carreaux	checked		
Ça me va?	Does it suit me?		
Ça ne me va pas.	It doesn't suit me.		

1 Find the odd word out in the following lists.

  a slip   culotte   veste   soutien-gorge   sous-vêtements

  b chaussures   baskets   sandales   bottes   chapeau

  c jupe   robe   pardessus   corsage   chemisier

  d maillot de bain   anorak   écharpe   gants   manteau

  e survêtement   chemise de nuit   jogging   baskets   short

2 Fill in the missing letters to find five words/phrases you might find on a clothes label.

  a l _ v _ g _   _ l _   m _ _ n   **d** c _ t _ n

  b l _ _ n _   **e** t _ _ l l _

  c n _ t t _ y _ g _   _ s _ c

3 Find nine colours in this wordsearch.

G	V	E	R	T	P	Q	Y	R
V	R	I	R	O	U	G	E	J
C	A	I	O	B	R	U	N	A
E	S	W	S	L	B	L	E	U
R	U	D	E	A	E	W	I	N
T	O	Q	C	N	P	T	X	E
I	N	U	J	C	A	E	E	B

4 Find a French word to fit each of these definitions.

  a Matching jacket and trousers.   **d** Alternative to buttons.

  b You wear it when it's raining.   **e** It holds your trousers up.

  c Everything you wear.

5 Solve the anagrams to find five words used to describe clothes.

    a frgiéf   **b** ungole   **c** éyear   **d** trocu   **e** torité

6 Complete the crossword to find six items of cold-weather clothing, and discover another one.

l'air	air	le monde	the world
*l'asthme	asthma	le pétrole	oil
*le bonheur	happiness	*le plomb	lead
le bruit	noise	*le préservatif	condom
*le cambriolage	burglary	*le réchauffement	warming
le camion	lorry	le sexe	sex
*le carton	cardboard	*le sida	aids
le centre de recyclage	recycling centre	le silence	silence
le changement	change	*un SDF (sans domicile fixe)	homeless person
*les chiffres (pl)	figures	*le taux	level/rate
le ciel	sky	le trottoir	pavement
le climat	climate	le trou	hole
le coup de soleil	sunburn	le verre	glass
*le crime	crime	le vol	theft
*le criminel	criminal		
les déchets (pl)	waste	*une allergie	allergy
*le détritus	rubbish	l'atmosphère	atmosphere
*l'éclairage	lighting	la catastrophe	catastrophe
*l'effet de serre	greenhouse effect	la circulation	traffic
		la cité	(housing) estate
*l'emballage	packaging	*la conséquence	consequence
un embouteillage	traffic jam	la conservation	conservation
l'environnement	environment	*la couche d'ozone	ozone layer
l'espace	space	la destruction	destruction
une espèce	species	l'énergie	energy
*l'espoir	hope	la faim	hunger
le gaz	gas	la fumée	smoke
*le gaz carbonique	carbon dioxide	*une inondation	flood
*les gaz (pl) d'échappement	exhaust gases	*la lumière	light
		la maladie	illness
*le logement	housing	*la pauvreté	poverty

la pollution	pollution	*à cause de	because of
la raison	reason	à peu près	nearly
la religion	religion	*affamé(e)	starving
*les ressources (pl)	resources	*ainsi	in this way
*la saleté	dirt	assez (de)	enough (of)
*la sécheresse	drought	atmosphérique	atmospheric
la source	source	autre	other
la terre	earth	*biodégradable	biodegradable
*la vague	wave	catholique	catholic
la violence	violence	compliqué(e)	complicated
la vitesse	speed	*en voie de disparition	endangered

arrêter	to stop	*épuisé(e)	exhausted
*avoir besoin (de)	to need	juif(ve)	jewish
avoir faim	to be hungry	musulman(e)	muslim
*avoir raison	to be right	naturel(le)	natural
*avoir tort	to be wrong	nécessaire	necessary
*cambrioler	to burgle	*nucléaire	nuclear
causer	to cause	*par conséquent	in consequence
comprendre	to understand	par terre	on the ground
conserver	to preserve	pollué(e)	polluted
*détruire	to destroy	protestant(e)	protestant
*épuiser	to exhaust, use up	*renouvelable	renewable
*éteindre	to put out (fire/light)	*respiratoire	breathing
faire attention	to be careful	solaire	solar
*gaspiller	to waste	vite	fast/quickly
jeter	to throw away		
recycler	to recycle		
*sauvegarder	to safeguard		
*trier	to sort		

1 Find a French word to match each of these definitions.

a Pattern of weather.

b Not having enough to eat.

c Person who has nowhere to live.

d The planet we live on.

e Not having enough money.

2 Find the odd word out in each of these lists.

a juif   catholique   nucléaire   protestant   musulman

b embouteillage   asthme   allergie   maladie   sida

c violence   cambriolage   vol   espoir   crime

d circulation   vitesse   gaz d'échappement   climat   camion

e sauvegarder   détruire   recycler   conserver   faire attention

3 Complete the following sentences with the appropriate adjective.

> atmosphérique   épuisées   en voie de disparition
> respiratoires   détritus

a Il faut sauvegarder les espèces ....

b La pollution .... est un grand problème.

c Il faut réduire la quantité de ....

d Il y a de plus en plus de maladies ....

e Les ressources naturelles seront bientôt ....

4 Fill in the missing vowels to find five 'green' words.

a r _ c y c l _ g _   c r _ n _ _ v _ l _ b l _   e n _ t _ r _ l

b b _ _ d _ g r _ d _ b l _   d _ n v _ r _ n n _ m _ n t

5 Find the opposite of each of these words/phrases.

  a avoir raison   **b** conserver   **c** simple   **d** malheur   **e** silence

6 Solve the anagrams to find five words to do with health.

  a speratifévr   **b** dialema   **c** thames   **d** leargeli   **e** puco de ilesol

7 Complete this environmental flow-chart.

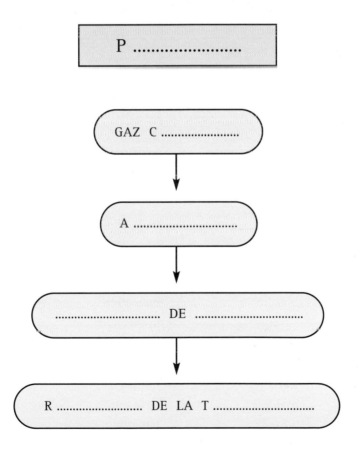

P ....

GAZ C ....

A ....

.... DE ....

R .... DE LA T ....

Time

*autrefois	in the past
*à la hâte	in a hurry
bientôt	soon
*de nouveau	again
déjà	already
dernier(ière)	last
encore (une fois)	(once) again
enfin	at last
ensuite	then
longtemps	for a long time
lorsque	when
parfois	sometimes
pendant	during
(plus) tard	late(r)
prochain(e)	next
*puis	then
quelquefois	sometimes
soudain	suddenly
tôt	early
*tout à coup	all of a sudden

Place

*ailleurs	elsewhere
au-dessous (de)	below
au-dessus (de)	above
arrière	back/rear
derrière	behind
devant	in front
*en bas	at the bottom/ downstairs
*en haut	at the top/ upstairs
ici	here
là(-bas)	(over) there
partout	everywhere
sous	under
sur	on
toutes directions	all routes
est	east
nord	north
ouest	west
sud	south

Argument

alors	then
*au contraire	on the contrary
un avantage	advantage
car	for/because
donc	so/therefore
faux(sse)	false
impossible	impossible
un inconvénient	disadvantage
mais	but
nécessaire	necessary
*obligatoire	compulsory
parce que	because
*par contre	on the other hand

par exemple	for example
peut-être	perhaps
plutôt	rather
possible	possible
pour	for/in order to
pourquoi	why
le problème	problem
*puisque	since
*quand même	even so
tout à fait	completely
vrai(e)	true

Negation

*ne ... aucun	not any
ne ... jamais	never
ne ... ni ... ni	neither ... nor
ne ... pas	not
ne ... personne	nobody/no-one
ne ... plus	no more/no longer
ne ... que	only
ne ... rien	nothing

Quantity/degree

aussi	also
la moitié	half
*pareil(le)	similar/same
peu	little
la plupart (de)	most (of)
plus (que)	more (than)
presque	almost
seulement	only
*tant	so much

*s'en aller	to go away
*avoir l'air	to seem/look like
comparer	to compare
croire	to think
*se dépêcher	to hurry
désirer	to want
dire	to say
parler	to speak
penser	to think
raconter	to tell (a story)
sourire	to smile
terminer	to finish
voir	to see
vouloir	to want

1 Self, Family & Friends

1 **a** oncle **b** neveu **c** femme
  d mari **e** fils

2 **a** ouvrier **b** secrétaire
  c célibataire **d** poisson
  e animal

3 **a** tante **b** oncle **b** grand-père
  d frère **e** nièce

4 **a** grands-parents **b** frères
  c animaux **d** travaille
  e parents

5 **a** copain - friend
  b correspondant - penfriend
  c prénom - first name
  d meilleur - best
  e lunettes - glasses

6 Animal: le chat, le cheval, le lapin
  le poisson rouge, la souris.

  Travail: un agent de police,
  le caissier, le chauffeur, le facteur
  la secrétaire.

  Famille: la belle-sœur, la cousine,
  le demi-frère, le mari, la tante.

7 **a** cheval **b** cobaye **c** poisson
  d souris **e** chien **f** lapin

8 bonjour   appelle   ans
  anniversaire   sœur   yeux
  cheveux   frère   appelle
  mignon

2 Local area and weather

1 **a** le bâtiment **b** le centre-ville
  c le soleil **d** le trajet

2 **a** collège **b** place **c** vacanciers
  d nuageux

3 le métro   la gare routière
  le musée   le bâtiment
  le grand magasin   la place
  la zone piétonne   le jardin public

4 **a** brouillard **b** neige **c** mauvais
  d pleut

5 **a** vieille **b** démuni **c** industrielle
  d historique **e** vieux

6 Magasins: le marché la boutique
  Chemin de fer: le train la gare
  le trajet la station
  La ville: le château le musée
  le jardin zoologique

7 ville   piétonne   boutiques
  magasins   touristes   musées
  monuments   magnifique   mer

8 **a** le château   le collège
  la cathédrale   **b** un estivant
  un habitant   le piéton   le touriste
  le vacancier   **c** un arbre
  le champ   le paysage   la colline
  la ferme

3 School life

1 **a** chimie **b** français **c** informatique
  d histoire **e** EPS **f** maths

2 **a** dessin **b** enseignement
  c faute **d** cartable **e** devoirs

3 trousse taille-crayon règle
  calculatrice gomme crayon

4 **a** neuf heures **b** une heure
  c 10 minutes **d** 15h30

5 magnétophone tableau papier

6 Positif : fort sympa intéressant
  Négatif : retenue difficile nul
  sévère barbant

7 **a** bavarder **b** dessine **c** passe
  d prêter

4 Education, careers and future plans

1 **a** apprenti **b** mécanicien
  c client **d** patron **e** avocate

2 **a** agresser **b** boucle d'oreille

3 Positif : enrichissant
  satisfaisant sûr bien payé
  Négatif : chômage violence
  racket démodé

4 **a** le marketing **b** la publicité
  c la médecine **d** le tourisme
  e le commerce

5 **a** continuer **b** rencontrer
  c perfectionner **d** écrire
  e gagner

6 **a** le racket **b** le maquillage
  c les bijoux **d** le vandalisme
  e les graffitis

7 **a** maçon **b** mécanicien
  c architecte **d** chômeur
  e agriculteur

8 **a** ingénieur **b** plombier
  c fonctionnaire **d** comptable
  e gendarme

5 Travel and transport

1 **a** carte **b** renseignements
  c avion **d** feux rouges
  e circulation **f** bicyclette

2 **a** aéroport **b** gare routière
  c station de métro **d** aire de
  repos **e** agence de voyages

3 Gare: composter votre billet
  deuxième classe SNCF

  Aéroport: piste vol AF218
  porte No8

  Station-service: essence faire le
  plein gazole sans plomb

4 **a** ceinture de sécurité **b** autoroute
  c consigne **d** direct **e** sortie

5 **a** en provenance de **b** départ
  c aller retour **d** monter dans
  e décoller

6 **a** circulation **b** réserver
  c wagon-restaurant
  d correspondance/changer
  e supplément

7 a bateau **b** aéroglisseur
c carte **d** hélicoptère **e** avion

6 Finding the way

1 a feux rouges gauche
b deuxième à droite **c** droite
carrefour **d** tout droit pont

2 a en face de **b** à côté de
c entre **d** devant

3 a derrière **b** avant
c loin (d'ici) **d** à gauche

7 Holidays, tourism & tourist information

1 a payant **b** ouvert **c** après-midi (or soir) **d** hiver

2 Au bord de la mer: scooter
ski nautique plongée sous-marine
planche à voile

En montagne: alpinisme ski
sports d'hiver

Mer ou montagne: photographie
excursion

3 a nuit **b** après-midi **c** balle
d parc **e** soir

4 a pique-nique **b** visite **c** bain
de soleil **d** excursion **e** alpinisme

5 randonnée paysage chaleur
bronzer caméscope côte
séjour nautique groupe
entrée tour

6 a all the year round
b pay accompanied (by an adult)
c allowed
d half-hour/30 minutes

8 Accommodation

1 a gîte **b** auberge de jeunesse
c camping **d** hôtel

2 a lampe de poche **b** poêle
c matelas **d** ouvre-boîte **e** tente

3 Hôtel: chambre de famille demi-pension grand lit

Camping: bloc sanitaire gaz
piquet sac de couchage

4 alimentation (food shop)
animation (entertainment)
caution (breakage deposit)
location (hire)
réception (reception)
réservation (reservation)

5 a prise (de courant) **b** 2 pièce
d'identité **c** matériel de camping
d pension complète

6 a passeport **b** tire-bouchon
c sale **d** poêle

7 a personne **b** location couchage
c chauffée **d** animé
e confirmer écrit

8 a descendre   faire   b garer
c réveiller   d marche (remember
to leave off the «r»).

9 People & places

1 a Pays Bas   b pays de Galles
c Belgique   d Etats-Unis
e Suisse OR Belgique

2 a le Canada   b les Alpes
c le Québec   d la région
e l'Angleterre

3 a écossaise   b indien
c canadienne   d belge

4 a Grande-Bretagne   b France
c Italie   d Allemagne
e Etats-Unis   f Japon

5 a population   b président
c francophone   d nationalité
e natal   f bilingue

6 Le Royaume-Uni: Irlande du Nord
Londres   Ecosse

La France: Normandie   Marseille
Rhône   Midi

L'Union européenne: Espagne
Portugal   Autriche   Bruxelles

Le monde: Quebec   Japon
Russie

7 a danois   b italienne
c écossais   d anglaise
e espagnol

10 Services (bank, post office, lost property)

1 a iii   b v   c i   d ii   e iv

2 a distributeur de billets
b porte-monnaie   c batterie
d formulaire   e portable

3 La Banque: chèque   billet de
100F/euros   livre sterling

La poste: timbre   code postal
paquet   lettre

France Télécom: télécarte   indicatif
portable

4 a timbre   b appel   c volant
d toucher

5 a bracelet   b parapluie
c montre   d paquet
e chéquier   f carte

6 a espèces   b crevé   c signer
d numéro   e portefeuille

7 a laisser   b argent   c cuir
d contenu   e perdu

11 Illness, accidents and injuries

1 cou   œil   cheville   bouche
bras   poignet   estomac   cœur
corps   nez

2 a pieds   b tête   c ordonnance
d comprimé   e hôpital

3 sang   centre hospitalier   radio
police   SAMU   blessure
pompier

4 **a** sparadrap   **b** médicament
c pastille   **d** sirop   **e** pilule

5 Médecin: rhume   mal de mer
fièvre   grippe

Hôpital: jambe cassée   crise
cardiaque

6 **a** trousse de premiers secours
b piqûre   **c** doigts   **d** entorse
e mal aux dents

7 **a** remède   **b** crise cardiaque
c orteil   **d** mort

12   House and home

1 **a** grenier   **b** deuxième étage
c premier étage   **d** rez-de-
chaussée   **e** cave

2 **a** rideau   **b** échelle   **c** terrasse
d moquette   **e** fenêtre

3 Cuisine: four   lave-vaisselle
cuisinière   congélateur

Salle de bains: baignoire   douche
lavabo

Salon: fauteuil   canapé   téléviseur

4 **a** garage   **b** lave-linge OR machine à
laver   **c** escalier   **d** cheminée
e réveil

5 **a** tapis   **b** escabeau   **c** miroir
d vestibule   **e** toilettes

6 **a** décorer   **b** partage   **c** déménage
d habite   **e** donne

7 **a** jardin   **b** antenne parabolique
c évier   **d** clé

13   Life at home

1 **a** se réveiller   se lever   se laver
se déshabiller   se coucher

b faire la cuisine   mettre la table
dîner   débarrasser la table   faire
la vaisselle

2 arroser les plantes   laver la voiture
sortir la poubelle   tondre le gazon
faire du jardinage

3 **a** souvent   **b** de temps en temps
c toujours   **d** rarement
e tous les jours

4 **a** se réveiller   **b** table   **c** argent
de poche   **d** jardinage

5 **a** me lève   **b** prépare   **c** demande
d reçois   **e** range

6 **a** poubelle   **b** table   **c** affaires
d lit   **e** gazon

7 **a** l'aspirateur   **b** brosse les dents
c le repassage   **d** un bain
e la vaisselle

14 Special occasions

1 **a** la Saint-Valentin **b** la fête nationale **c** le jour de Noël **d** la Saint-Sylvestre

2 **a** anniversaire **b** Noël **c** mariage OR noces

3 **a** Bonne année **b** Bon appétit **c** Bon anniversaire **d** Félicitations **e** Bon voyage **f** Joyeux Noël

4 **a** klaxonnent **b** cadeaux **c** feu d'artifice **d** en chocolat **e** carte

5 **a** garçon d'honneur **b** noces d'argent **c** Santé/à la tienne/à la vôtre **d** fête des Mères **e** alliance

6 **a** mairie **b** champagne **c** mariée **d** vin **e** mari **f** religieuse **g** église **h** mariage

7 **a** fête **b** recevoir **c** envoie **d** ouvrir **e** fait la bise

15 Food & drink

1 Fruit: fraise poire citron pamplemousse

Légume: pomme de terre petits pois épinards poireau

Viande: poulet agneau bœuf saucisson

2 **a** limonade **b** sardine **c** agneau **d** chocolat

3 Potage: poivre oignon pâtes pommes de terre sel

Gâteau: œufs sucre fruits farine confiture

4 **a** faim **b** végétarien(ne) **c** aime **d** allergique

5 un œuf le thon le lait le yaourt

6 **a** v **b** i **c** iv **d** iii **e** ii

7 concombre laitue huile oignons œufs tomates

16 Eating out

1 **a** café-crème **b** entrecôte **c** dessert **d** légume **e** melon

2 **a** iii **b** i **c** v **d** ii **e** iv

3 **a** hors-d'œuvre **b** côte de porc **c** tarte maison **d** compris **e** service

4 **a** pourboire **b** apéritif **c** croque-monsieur **d** nature **e** saignant

5 **a** carte **b** commander **c** pour commencer **d** monsieur **e** plat principal **f** boisson **g** bouteille

6 **a** pizza **b** hamburger
c sandwich **d** crêpe **e** casse-croûte

7 addition pourboire cuiller tasse assiette verre couvert

17 Healthy living

1 **a** fumez éviter **b** alcool
c crise cardiaque **d** dangereux
e refuser **f** en forme régime

2 **a** santé **b** sport **c** exercice
d équilibré

3 **a** athlète **b** adolescent **c** drogué

4 **a** malheureux **b** inadmissible
c imprudent **d** lent **e** dangereux

18 The world of work

1 **a** emploi **b** salaire **c** employé
d conférence **e** journal

2 **a** chanteur **b** employé
c ouvrier **d** boucher **e** coiffeur
f directeur **g** informaticien

3 **a** disquette **b** photocopie
c fiche **d** clavier **e** logiciel

4 **a** licenciement **b** formation
c usine **d** entretien **e** contrat
f équipe

5 **a** boucher **b** employée
c fermier **d** actrice **e** coiffeur
f mannequin **g** électricien
h épicier

6 **a** Allô **b** directeur **c** part
d quittez **e** rappeler

7 **a** salaire **b** augmenter
c économies **d** fric

19 Leisure activities

1 **a** escrime **b** échecs **c** handball
d cartes **e** volley

2 flûte violon batterie trompette piano guitare

3 **a** lecture **b** photographie
c voile **d** cyclisme
e promenade

4 **a** fana(tique) **b** doué
c favori/préféré **d** passionnante
e sportif/sportive

5 **a** patin à roulettes **b** piscine
c concert **d** passe-temps

6 **a** avoir lieu **b** nager **c** écouter
d lire **e** danser

7 **a** musicien **b** alpinisme OR ski
c match **d** patinoire

20 Media (cinema, television, theatre)

1 Télévision: téléspectateur
informations sous-titre feuilleton

Théâtre: scène pièce balcon
applaudir

2 **a** place **b** radio **c** courrier du cœur **d** image **e** caméra

3 a épouvante b comiques
  c amour d sous-titrés
  e en noir et blanc

4 a émission b documentaire
  c publicité d série e chaîne

5 a courrier du cœur b jeu télévisé
  c vedette d dessin animé
  e presse

6 horreur western épouvante
  comiques policier amour
  aventures

7 a salle b polar c écran
  d sous-titre e balcon

21 People & personalities

1 Positif: aimable généreux génial
  charmant courageux

  Négatif: cruel méchant stupide
  égoïste paresseux

2 a héros b joueur c champion
  d femme e peintre f homme

3 a disputé b gagné c marqué
  d ressemble e critiquent
  f fâchent

4 a timide b intelligent c poli
  d haine e laid

5 a comportement b sens de
  l'humour c enfance d date de
  naissance e rapports

6 a accueillant b branché
  c dynamique d ouvert
  e honnête

7 a jaloux b pénible c cruel
  d égoïste e bizarre

22 Meeting people

1 a août b aujourd'hui c soir
  d instant e Au revoir
  f Bienvenue

2 a fixer un rendez-vous b saluer
  c être sur le point de ...
  d aller chercher e manquer

3 a accepter b décidé
  c embrassée d proposé
  e remercié

4 a à l'heure b dans cinq minutes
  c à quelle heure d ce matin
  e le lendemain

5 a avant-hier b hier matin
  c cet après-midi d demain soir
  e après-demain

6 a certainement b à bientôt
  c avec plaisir d d'accord
  e ravi merci

7 a salut b demain c bien sûr
  d passerai te chercher e à demain
  f merci

23 Shopping

1 **a** comptoir   **b** chariot
   c boucherie   **d** monnaie   **e** léger

2 **a** iii   **b** v   **c** iv   **d** i   **e** ii

3 **a** supermarché   **b** pharmacie
   c librairie   **d** épicerie   **e** boucherie
   f crémerie   **g** marché

4 **a** platine laser   **b** caméscope
   c jeu de société   **d** appareil photo
   e enveloppe

5 **a** heures d'affluence   **b** faire un
   paquet-cadeau   **c** fermeture annuelle
   d opticien   **e** dégustation

6 **a** réduction   **b** pour le prix de
   deux   **c** promotion   **d** achetez
   e gratuit

7 **a** affreux   **b** réduit   **c** fraîche
   d d'occasion   **e** bon marché

24 Fashion and clothes

1 **a** veste   **b** chapeau   **c** pardessus
   d maillot de bain   **e** chemise de
   nuit

2 **a** lavage à la main   **b** laine
   c nettoyage à sec   **d** coton
   e taille

3 vert   gris   rose   blanc
   rouge   jaune   brun
   violet   bleu

4 **a** costume   **b** imper(méable)
   c vêtements   **d** fermeture éclair
   e ceinture

5 **a** griffé   **b** longue   **c** rayée
   d court   **e** étroit

6 **a** blouson   **b** anorak   **c** gants
   d manteau   **e** écharpe
   f pardessus   **g** bottes

25 Current affairs and social issues

1 **a** climat   **b** faim   **c** SDF (sans
   domicile fixe)   **d** terre
   e pauvreté/pauvre

2 **a** nucléaire   **b** embouteillage
   c espoir   **d** climat   **e** détruire

3 **a** en voie de disparition
   b atmosphérique   **c** détritus
   d respiratoires   **e** épuisées

4 **a** recyclage   **b** biodégradable
   c renouvelable   **d** environnement
   e naturel

5 **a** avoir tort   **b** jeter/détruire/
   gaspiller   **c** compliqué   **d** bonheur
   e bruit

6 **a** préservatif   **b** maladie
   c asthme   **d** allergie   **e** coup de
   soleil

7 pollution
   gaz carbonique
   atmosphère
   effet de serre
   réchauffement de la terre